SOLUTIONS FOR A CLEANER, GREENER PLANET

ENVIRONMENTAL CHEMISTRY

MARC ZIMMER

TWENTY-FIRST CENTURY BOOKS / MINNEAPOLIS

To all my students

Twenty-First Century Books
A division of Lerner Publishing Group, Inc.
241 First Avenue North
Minneapolis, MN 55401 USA

For reading levels and more information, look up this title at www.lernerbooks.com.

Main body text set in Adrianna 10/15.
Typeface provided by Chank Foundry.

Library of Congress Cataloging-in-Publication Data

Names: Zimmer, Marc, author.
Title: Solutions for a cleaner, greener planet : environmental chemistry / Marc Zimmer.
Description: Minneapolis : Twenty-First Century Books, 2019. | Includes bibliographical references and index. |
Identifiers: LCCN 2018010574 (print) | LCCN 2018040787 (ebook) | ISBN 9781541543966 (eb pdf) | ISBN 9781541519794 (lb : alk. paper)
Subjects: LCSH: Environmental chemistry. | Teenagers—Conduct of life.
Classification: LCC TD193 (ebook) | LCC TD193 .Z56 2019 (print) | DDC 577.27—dc23

LC record available at https://lccn.loc.gov/2018010574

Manufactured in the United States of America
1-44315-34561-8/14/2018

CONTENTS

CHAPTER 1

HEAVY METALS

Did you know that atoms are so small that if we took all the atoms in a cup of water and made them the size of a marble, Earth would be covered in more than 50 miles (80 km) of marbles? Atoms are the building blocks of all matter on Earth, and understanding atoms is central to modern life. Through chemistry—the study of atoms and chemical processes—researchers are able to do many things. They can design new medicines, make smaller and longer-lasting batteries, and improve fuel efficiencies of cars, planes, and other vehicles.

While chemical processes can make our lives easier and more fun, they can also pollute the environment around us. Our shared planet faces many environmental challenges. Understanding the chemistry that underlies these issues is a key part of coming up with solutions. The field of environmental chemistry focuses on understanding the most common pollutants; how they pollute; how they get into our food, water, and air; and what the consequences to human, plant, and animal health are. Just as critical is that environmental chemistry also focuses on solutions.

Astronauts aboard *Apollo 17* took this famous photo of Earth, known as the Blue Marble, in 1972. It created a global awareness of the fragility of Earth and helped fuel the environmental movement.

DOWN TO BASICS

Atoms are tiny spheres composed of three types of subatomic particles. In the center of each sphere is an incredibly small nucleus. The nucleus is made of neutrons (with no electrical charge) and protons (with a positive charge). Whizzing around the nucleus are negatively charged electrons. All atoms are neutral and have no overall electrical charge. They have equal numbers of protons and electrons. But every element has a different number of subatomic particles. Hydrogen has the fewest, with just one proton, one electron, and zero neutrons. At the other extreme is oganesson, which has 118 protons, 118 electrons, and 176 neutrons. The number of protons and the number of electrons in an atom is the atomic number, often abbreviated as the letter Z. The atomic mass number, A, is the combined number of protons and the neutrons. For oganesson, $Z = 118$ and $A = 294$. For hydrogen, A and Z are both 1.

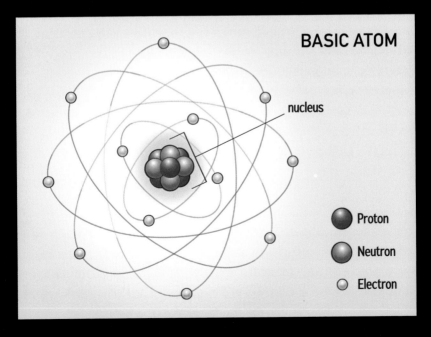

BASIC ATOM

nucleus

Proton

Neutron

Electron

The basic subatomic particles of an atom are protons, neutrons, and electrons. Each chemical element, from hydrogen to oganesson, has a different number of subatomic particles.

Russian chemist Dmitri Mendeleev organized his periodic table by the properties and mass of known elements at the time. He understood that the physical and chemical properties of elements were related to their atomic mass. So he put groups of similar elements in the same vertical columns. His table was so accurate that it predicted the existence and properties of elements that had yet to be discovered and allowed room to insert them once they were.

In 1869 Russian chemist Dmitri Mendeleev published a groundbreaking infographic. At the time, scientists knew of about fifty-six types of chemical elements. But no one had come up with a good way to arrange them into an easy, practical table. Mendeleev came up with a very elegant and useful visual way of organizing all the known elements. Even though it was not immediately accepted, his ideas formed the basis of the modern periodic table.

In the periodic table, each of the elements in a particular column, also called a group, or family, is abbreviated by a one- or two-letter symbol. The periodic table has eighteen groups. Each of the elements is numbered, referring to the number of protons in that atom's nucleus. This number is called the element's atomic number (Z). The elements in each group have similar properties. For example, lithium (Li), sodium (Na), potassium (K), rubidium (Rb), cesium (Cs), and francium (Fr) are in group 1. They are all solids that react violently with water. On the far side of the periodic table is group 18 with helium (He), neon (Ne), argon (Ar), krypton (Kr), xenon (Xe), and radon (Rn). They are all unreactive gases. Oganesson is also in group 18, but it is synthetic (manufactured by humans) and only exists for a fraction of a second.

The periodic table is also divided into three main sections—metals, nonmetals, and metalloids. Metals make up most of Earth's known atoms and are in the center of the table. Metals conduct heat and electricity and melt at very high temperatures. Some of the metals in the lower portions of the periodic table are very dense and are called the heavy metals. For example, mercury (Hg) is 13.5 times denser than water, and lead is 11.3 times denser than water. Mercury is the only liquid metal. It is so dense that a laptop would float on top of liquid mercury. Some of the heavy metals, such as mercury, lead, and arsenic, are very toxic. Other heavy metals, such as silver, gold, and ruthenium, are relatively harmless.

The modern periodic table is based on the infographic that Dmitri Mendeleev came up with in the nineteenth century. In this version, metals are shown in the yellow boxes, metalloids in red, and nonmetals in green. The symbols for synthetic elements, which are created in labs, are white with black outlining.

Some metals such as iron, zinc, and cobalt are essential nutrients, and we would die without them in our diet.

Nonmetals are on the right side of the table. They do not conduct heat and electricity and tend to be brittle solids. Examples of nonmetals are sulfur, carbon, and silicon. Metalloids are elements that resemble both metals and nonmetals. They look like metals and are shiny. But they behave like nonmetals because they don't conduct electricity and are brittle.

In the twenty-first century, scientists know of 118 different elements. Although 24 have to be synthesized in the lab, 94 of them occur naturally. The naturally occurring elements are the building blocks of everything we see around us in the natural world, from plants (mainly made up of C, N, P, and O) to cars (Fe, C, and Al). The synthetic elements—white outlined in black in the periodic table include everything from technetium to oganesson.

How can so few elements make up the splendid diversity of our world? They do it by combining with other elements. Think of the twenty-six letters of the English alphabet and the way we combine them with one another to form words and sentences. Then we use them to create poetry, plays, novels, textbooks, social media postings, and more. Similarly, when atoms of two or more elements combine, they form a compound. This compound will have completely different properties from the elements that combined to make it. Water is a familiar compound. Made up of two hydrogen atoms and one oxygen atom, its chemical abbreviation, or formula, is H_2O.

LEAD ALERT!

One of the most common elements in nature is lead. Lead has atomic number 82. That means it has eighty-two electrons and eighty-two protons. Its most common form has 126 neutrons in the nucleus. The chemical symbol for lead is Pb—from *plumbum*, the

CHEMICAL FORMULAS

A molecular, or chemical, formula shows the total number of atoms of each element in one molecule of a substance. For example, the chemical formula for water is H_2O. This means that each water molecule has three atoms total. Two of those atoms are hydrogen (H), and one is oxygen (O). In the formula for water, you can tell that water has only one oxygen atom because the formula has no number after the O. White arsenic, As_2O_3, has two arsenic (As) atoms and three oxygen atoms. How many atoms does H_3PO_4 have?

Latin word for "lead." It is easy to extract from the ores, or rocks, in which it naturally occurs. Lead is soft and malleable, and it melts at 620°F (327°C). That's a very low melting point for a metal. All these properties make it very easy to work with. So some of the world's earliest civilizations extracted lead for making metal figures and pots.

However, ancient peoples also knew that lead could be toxic if they consumed it. For example, the ancient Greeks knew that drinking acidic beverages that were stored in lead containers or that flowed through lead pipes could cause illness. So they avoided lead cooking utensils and made their plumbing pipes out of clay. The ancient Romans used lead to make pipes and cooking vessels and to weatherproof their houses. Many of these artifacts are seen in Italian museums and ruins.

Some historians believe Roman civilization collapsed because of neurological problems among the ruling class caused by lead poisoning. For example, lead acetate is a sweet-tasting lead compound also known as sugar of lead. The ruling class of the ancient Roman world was very fond of wine and drank up to three bottles a day per person. Roman winemakers were not yet expert at their craft, and the wine they made didn't taste very good. To hide its imperfections and to make the wine taste better, they added a sweetener. It contained significant amounts of lead acetate. Some historians suggest that the decline of the Roman Empire in the fifth century CE was brought about by leaders drinking too much wine and being poisoned over time by lead acetate. Records show that members of the upper classes often suffered from dementia, infertility, and organ failure—all symptoms of lead poisoning. Chemical analysis of the bones of ancient Roman skeletons shows that the bones contain about one hundred times more lead than those of twenty-first-century human bones. Together, these pieces of evidence strongly support the lead-poisoning theory of the decline of the empire.

Historians also point to a gruesome side of ancient Roman history. Sometimes lead was used to poison people. For example, rumors circulated at the time of his death that Pope Clement II—who served as the head of the Roman Catholic Church from 1046 to 1047—had been poisoned with sugar of lead. In 1959 chemist and criminologist Walter Specht (working for the Bavarian State Bureau of Investigation in Germany) performed a chemical analysis of the pope's bones. Specht confirmed that lead poisoning caused his death. The pope liked wine, and possibly someone placed lead acetate in a cup of wine to deliver the lethal dose.

Another more famous lead poisoning—though not intentional—contributed to the tragic fate of the 1845 Franklin Expedition across the Arctic. Captain Sir John Franklin of England and his team set out that year to find a waterway passage, known as the Northwest Passage, across the Arctic. However, Franklin and 128 crew members aboard the HMS *Erebus* and HMS *Terror* became icebound near King William Island in the Canadian Arctic. The British government offered a large reward to save the men, and numerous search parties launched ships to find them. The rescue crews discovered graves and artifacts from the ships on King William Island. The expedition was one of the first to use newly invented tin cans to store meat and soup for the long journey. Lead solder joined the seams in the cans together. In 1981 forensic analysis of the bones of the remains of the sailors found in graves on King William Island revealed that they had very high lead concentrations. Experts believe this could very well have contributed to their deaths.

SYMPTOMS OF LEAD POISONING

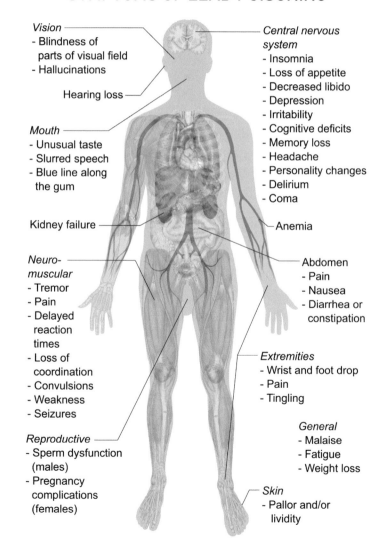

Vision
- Blindness of parts of visual field
- Hallucinations

Hearing loss

Mouth
- Unusual taste
- Slurred speech
- Blue line along the gum

Kidney failure

Neuro-muscular
- Tremor
- Pain
- Delayed reaction times
- Loss of coordination
- Convulsions
- Weakness
- Seizures

Reproductive
- Sperm dysfunction (males)
- Pregnancy complications (females)

Central nervous system
- Insomnia
- Loss of appetite
- Decreased libido
- Depression
- Irritability
- Cognitive deficits
- Memory loss
- Headache
- Personality changes
- Delirium
- Coma

Anemia

Abdomen
- Pain
- Nausea
- Diarrhea or constipation

Extremities
- Wrist and foot drop
- Pain
- Tingling

General
- Malaise
- Fatigue
- Weight loss

Skin
- Pallor and/or lividity

The Canadian Victoria Strait Expedition finally located the wreckage of HMS *Erebus* in 2014 at the bottom of the ocean west of O'Reilly Island. In 2016 the Arctic Research Foundation expedition found the wreck of HMS *Terror* south of King William Island in Terror Bay.

THE DANGERS OF LEAD

For any material to have a negative effect on the health of an organism, it has to enter the organism somehow. People can ingest lead (take it into the body) through food and water. Or if it is airborne—in dust from leaded paint or in gasoline fumes—they breathe it into their lungs. Once lead enters the body, it circulates in the blood until the blood is so full of lead that it becomes saturated and no more lead can dissolve in the blood. The body then deposits the lead in its soft tissues, especially in the brain. Lead and calcium atoms are similar in size and have similar chemical characteristics. So lead can also take the place of calcium in bones, where it can stay for decades until the bones start dissolving and weakening with old age.

If lead stayed in the blood and bones, it would be harmless. But the lead in the body's soft tissues causes toxic effects. Babies and children are especially vulnerable to the toxic effects of lead. Their brains are rapidly growing, and lead poisoning interferes with brain development. Numerous studies have shown consistent and harmful neurological damage associated with lead exposure that happens shortly before and after birth. The lead poisoning reduces the attention span, increases violent behavior, and compromises intelligence. These permanent changes lead to difficulties at school and work. Lead can be lethal. Experts at the Institute for Health Metrics and Evaluation at the University of Washington in Seattle believe that globally more than 494,550 deaths were caused by lead poisoning in 2015. Many of these deaths come much later in life and are due to high blood pressure and heart disease.

Lead abatement projects are meant to permanently eliminate existing lead-based paint. If they know they have a lead problem, homeowners will sometimes voluntarily hire expert teams such as this one. The average lead-removal project costs about $10,000. In lead-poisoning and other cases, a state or local government will require abatement.

LEAD IN PAINT

Many lead compounds have brilliant, stable colors. So manufacturers use them in paints. Lead chromate creates the bright yellow color used to paint school buses. It is also in the yellow stripes that mark lanes on roads or no parking zones on curbsides. A lead carbonate compound called white lead has been used to make massive amounts of very durable bright white paint. Painters in the United States often used it to paint the insides of houses. Over time, the paint would occasionally peel off in flecks. The lead in the paint was sweet tasting, so the flecks were appealing snacks to young children and crawling babies—the age at which people are most vulnerable to lead poisoning. In 1977 the United States banned the use of lead paint in residential properties although it's still used for yellow road markings. Canada and the countries of the European Union also banned lead paint. So far, sixty-eight countries have banned lead paint. Environmental regulations in Africa are much less strict, and only three countries on that continent have banned it.

FINDING ALTERNATIVES FOR LEAD PAINT

Laws are one way to control pollution and the harmful effects of toxic products on people. The Clean Air Act and the Clean Water Act are the two main pieces of federal legislation in the United States that help control the amount of pollutants that humans release into the environment. The Clean Air Act of 1963 was the first federal law in the United States to regulate air pollution. The Clean Water Act became law in 1972. Congress has amended, or changed, both laws numerous times. The Environmental Protection Agency (EPA)—created in 1970—carries out the regulations of both the Clean Air and Clean Water Acts. Laws, regulations, and the threat of lawsuits usually spur industries and researchers to find alternatives that either reduce or prevent the release of pollutants into the environment. With the election of Donald Trump as president of the United States in 2016, he, his staff, and some other lawmakers have worked to deregulate pollution standards, to relax the Clean Air and Clean Water Acts, and generally to allow more pollution. They feel—and some businesses agree—that the changes will stimulate the economy. Many other Americans disagree strongly. They fear the changes will be too risky for Earth's fragile environment.

Cities and counties also can make their own rules to deal with pollution. For example, in 1951 Baltimore, Maryland, became the first city in the United States to ban the use of lead paint in the interior of houses. By the 1970s, the use of lead paints had decreased dramatically across the country. In 1977 the federal government banned the indoor use of white lead paint and the use of lead paints on toys and indoor furniture.

A naturally occurring pigment called titanium white is the most common substitute for lead-based white paints. It has some disadvantages when compared to lead-based paints. It is not as durable, so painters often coat it with layers of silicon or aluminum oxide to protect it. When mixed with other paints, it has a chalky color and consistency. It is also difficult to mix with other colors because its color can dominate. But its huge advantage is that it is not toxic. It is so safe it is used in food colorings, sunscreen, and for the white color of many toothpastes.

LEAD IN GASOLINE

The gasoline that fuels cars is a petroleum product. It is the most valuable component of the black viscous (thick) crude oil that oil wells extract from the earth. Refining is the process of separating the components of crude oil. Pure gasoline from crude oil tends to ignite too quickly in a car engine because the naturally occurring octane in crude oil is highly flammable. It will burn before a car's spark plugs fire. Then the car engine knocks, or pings, and doesn't perform efficiently.

Refineries assign an octane rating, typically 87 or 91, to the petroleum they produce. The number indicates how easily the fuel ignites. The lower the number the more easily it ignites. If it ignites too easily, the engine knocks. So, starting in the 1920s, refineries began to add tetraethyllead—a chemical octane booster—to gasoline sold in the United States. But from the very beginning, gasoline companies began noticing alarming effects of the lead additive on workers. For example, the Standard Oil tetraethyllead

In the early part of the twentieth century, refineries routinely added a chemical called tetraethyllead, or ethyl, to gasoline. The lead additive improved engine performance. Ads such as this one from England in the 1930s suggested that ethyl not only promoted a car's performance. It also made it and its owners more desirable.

production plant in Bayway, New Jersey, was one of the first factories to make tetraethyllead for octane-enhanced gasoline. The workers in the building began behaving abnormally. They became moody and short-tempered, had difficulties sleeping, and couldn't remember their friend's names. The plant was known as the "loony gas building," and by November 1924, thirty-two of the forty-nine workers in the lead additive production plant had been hospitalized. Five workers died from lead poisoning before the plant launched safety procedures to limit the exposure of their workers to lead. But gasoline companies continued using lead to lower the octane rating of their fuel even though they knew the lead additive was toxic.

Refineries were adding about 0.13 ounces of the lead compound per gallon (1 gram per L) of fuel. By 1970 they were adding 360,000 tons (327,600 t) of lead each year to gasoline. As the fuel and additives burned in car engines, most of the lead was released in the exhaust fumes. On average, a person breathes 3,000 gallons (11,360 L) of air each day. In 1970 this air contained tiny but unhealthy amounts of lead.

Studies then showed that airborne lead reduces human fertility and negatively impacts cognitive abilities, or general intelligence. Later studies conducted in 2007 also showed a strong correlation in cities all over the world between the amount of lead gasoline used and the amount of violent crimes recorded in that city two decades later. The delay was factored in so researchers could observe over time the behavior of people exposed to lead when they were babies and children. In US cities in which the use of leaded gasoline was discontinued quickly, violent crime decreased quickly years later. But in cities in which leaded gasoline was faded out slowly, a corresponding decrease in crime took much longer. Brain scans have revealed that lead poisoning damages the parts of the brain responsible for aggression control, which could explain these observations.

FINDING ALTERNATIVES FOR LEADED GASOLINE

The EPA was founded in 1970. One of its first campaigns was to phase out leaded gasoline. Refineries responded and by the mid-1970s, unleaded gasoline was available alongside leaded gas at most gas stations in the United States. In 1996 the Clean Air Act prohibited the sale of leaded gasoline for on-road vehicles in the United States. With the ban, the levels of lead in the blood of American children between the ages of one and five dropped by more than 80 percent from 1976 to 1999. Barry Commoner, a

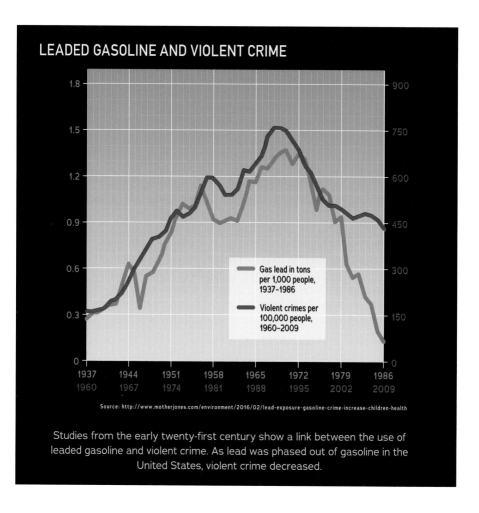

LEADED GASOLINE AND VIOLENT CRIME

Gas lead in tons per 1,000 people, 1937–1986

Violent crimes per 100,000 people, 1960–2009

Source: http://www.motherjones.com/environment/2016/02/lead-exposure-gasoline-crime-increase-children-health

Studies from the early twenty-first century show a link between the use of leaded gasoline and violent crime. As lead was phased out of gasoline in the United States, violent crime decreased.

biologist and one of the founders of the American environmental movement, has called the elimination of leaded gasoline, "one of the [few] environmental success stories." As of 2017, the nations of Algeria, Yemen, and Iraq are the only countries that still use leaded gasoline.

With the ban on lead, refineries had to figure out a new way to prevent gasoline from igniting too early. So instead of lead, they began using an additive called methyl tertiary butyl ether (MTBE).

At the time, it didn't seem to be toxic. And exhaust from gas with MTBE did not contribute to smog (airborne pollution) or to ground-level ozone formation. Both of these contribute to respiratory diseases. However, MTBE from gasoline leaks and spills has contaminated important groundwater sources. So refineries in the United States are phasing out MTBE, although it is commonly used in gasoline in Europe and in Asia. In the United States, refineries use corn-based ethanol instead of MTBE. Most gasoline sold in the United States contains 10 percent by volume of ethanol to prevent knocking. Next time you are at a gas station check out the information posted at the pump. What is the octane rating of the gas, and what are the additives?

Barry Commoner was a biologist, ecologist, and major voice of the environmental movement in the 1960s and 1970s. He warned of the dangers of nuclear weapons testing. He was an early supporter of recycling, organic food, and reducing dependence on fossil fuels. He saw environmentalism as a political issue and ran (unsuccessfully) for president in 1980 as a Citizens Party candidate.

LEAD IN WATER PIPES

In the late nineteenth century, US cities began installing large-scale sanitation systems to bring clean water and indoor plumbing to homes and businesses. Builders knew that lead was toxic. But they used lead pipes anyway because they were easy to work with and didn't leak. Lead was also less expensive than copper or bronze, and

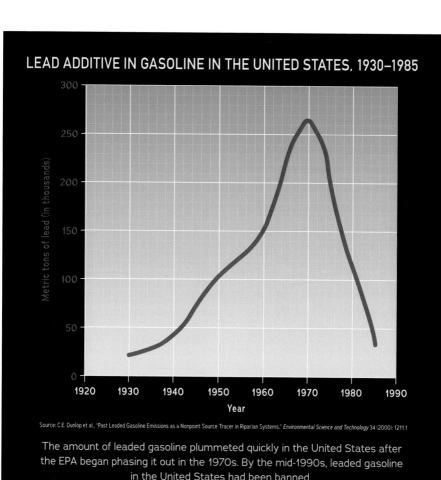

LEAD ADDITIVE IN GASOLINE IN THE UNITED STATES, 1930–1985

Source: C.E. Dunlop et al., "Past Leaded Gasoline Emissions as a Nonpoint Source Tracer in Riparian Systems," *Environmental Science and Technology* 34 (2000): 1211.1

The amount of leaded gasoline plummeted quickly in the United States after the EPA began phasing it out in the 1970s. By the mid-1990s, leaded gasoline in the United States had been banned.

plastics were not mass-produced until World War II (1939–1945). Chicago, Illinois, for example, laid 75 miles (121 km) of lead pipes every year between 1890 and 1920. With amendments to the Safe Drinking Water Act in 1986, the EPA prohibited the installation of lead water pipes nationwide. Many US homes built before that year are therefore likely to contain lead pipes and lead fixtures. Usually this isn't a problem. The water that flows through the pipes often contains minerals that form a deposit in the pipes. Over time, the deposit builds up enough to prevent the water from contacting the lead. If the water does not contain these minerals, water treatment plants will add them.

THE CRISIS IN FLINT

In April 2014, the City of Flint, Michigan, decided to discontinue purchasing its water from Detroit. Detroit draws its water from Lake Huron and the Detroit River and sells some of it to other cities. Flint was once a booming General Motors (GM) auto-manufacturing town. But when GM downsized in the 1980s, the town's economy suffered greatly. Leaders wanted to save money, so in 2014, they decided to draw the city's water at less cost from the nearby Flint River. This water is slightly more acidic than the water from Lake Huron. It rapidly ate away the protective mineral layer that had formed a barrier between the lead pipes and Flint's drinking water. Residents began to report that the water looked, smelled, and tasted odd. Tests done the next year by the EPA and Virginia Polytechnic Institute and Michigan State University found dangerous levels of lead in the city's drinking water. More than one hundred thousand people in Flint were exposed to excessive lead concentrations. They experienced delayed puberty, hearing and cognitive problems, and behavioral disorders. And some of the excessive lead in the drinking water bound to chlorine in the water, preventing the chlorine from disinfecting the water. This caused an outbreak of Legionnaires' disease in Flint in 2014 to 2015.

The residents of Flint and city leaders were aware they were facing a crisis. Yet incompetence, political infighting, and a fear of lawsuits slowed down action to solve the problem. Flint leaders didn't switch back until October 2015 to buying the city's water from Detroit. The city also added phosphates to its water to build up a replacement protective layer between the lead and the water. Residents and leaders knew that it would take time to flush

The National Guard helped distribute clean, safe drinking water to residents in Flint, Michigan, during the worst of the drinking water crisis.

all the lead out of the city's water system. They also knew that health problems caused by the lead were permanent. Clean water wouldn't undo the damage.

The Flint environmental disaster is an example of environmental injustice. Manufacturing industries, landfills, garbage incinerators, and other highly polluting industries are much more likely to be in or close to poor neighborhoods. Industries know that if they target an affluent (wealthy) neighborhood, residents will call on attorneys, politicians, and scientists to prevent the industries from building near the wealthy areas. Transporting garbage, electronics waste, and hazardous wastes from wealthy to less affluent towns or from the United States to poor, developing countries in Africa is another example of environmental injustice.

The residents of Flint are not wealthy, and almost 60 percent are black. If Flint had not had economic problems, the city probably wouldn't have looked for a source of less expensive water. Even if it had, better prepared leadership would have tested the water for lead. Lead tests are standard in many cities and inexpensive.

Many critics also point out that Michigan authorities would have responded to the crisis much more quickly had the city's population been white and more affluent.

FINDING ALTERNATIVES FOR LEAD PIPES

Estimates show that the US water system has between six and a half million to ten million lead pipes. To replace all those pipes would cost between $16 billion and $18 billion. Since the mid-1980s, builders, municipalities (cities), and water companies no longer install lead plumbing. They no longer use lead solder to connect pipes. However, the US government and individual cities and counties don't have laws to remove existing lead plumbing. The EPA does have the Lead and Copper Rule. It requires water utility companies to sample water that comes out of household taps for lead and copper contamination. The tests are conducted every three years on homes that are the most likely to have lead soldering or pipes.

Modern pipes are made of plastic, steel, or copper. Ideally, safe pipes would replace all the lead pipes in the nation. Because of the costs—in the billions of dollars—this is not always realistic, especially for poor communities. So instead, many water utility companies are inserting additives into the water. These additives, mainly orthophosphate, prevent corrosion and keep lead from contaminating drinking water.

WHAT CAN YOU DO?

About twenty-four million housing units built before 1978 in the United States have chipping lead paint and lead dust. Children under six living in these homes are particularly vulnerable to lead paint. They should be kept away from the peeling paint, and their hands should be washed regularly. Floors and windows should be cleaned with a wet mop or a wet rag every two or three weeks.

Thanks to the Safe Drinking Water Act, lead is no longer a major pollutant in drinking water. But some homes with old pipe fittings, older fixtures, or lead solder may have it. The only way to know is to test the water. You can't smell or taste lead in water. According to the Centers for Disease Control and Prevention, you should ask your water provider whether your home water has lead in it. If it does, most likely it is in the hot water tap. Don't drink or cook with water that comes from the hot water tap if you suspect lead is in the water. Don't drink from the tap at all until you have let it run for a few minutes. Bathing or showering in water that contains lead is usually safe.

ARSENIC ALERT!

From a sign of wealth to a popular poison, arsenic has an intriguing history. From ancient Roman times through the Middle Ages (ca. 500–1500), arsenic compounds were commonly used as a poison, particularly in royal intrigues. At much lower concentrations, people also used arsenic therapeutically to treat sleeping sickness and leukemia. Even in the twenty-first century, about fifty drugs used in China still contain arsenic.

When people think of arsenic as a poison (arsenic trioxide, or As_2O_3), they often think of crime novels. Yet arsenic poisoning is the stuff of real life. For example, Giulia Tofana is among the most famous poisoners in history. In the seventeenth century, she invented an arsenic-based product called Aqua Tofana (Tofana's water). She made it with her daughter and three helpers and sold it openly to women in Palermo, Sicily, where she lived. Tofana sold it under the guise of a cosmetic and a skin lightener. She mainly sold it to women trapped in abusive marriages. She explained to them that four doses of the clear and tasteless poison in wine or food were enough to kill a man. Early symptoms of the slow impact of arsenic poisoning resemble a cold or flu. Later stages mimic the effects of cholera, which was common then. These symptoms include diarrhea, stomach cramps, nausea, dark urine, and dehydration. One of Tofana's customers reported her to the authorities. Tofana was popular among the local population, so she was difficult to track down. She was eventually arrested. Under torture, she confessed to helping in the arsenic murder of six hundred men. Tofana, her daughter, and the three helpers were sentenced to death for murder. All five were executed in Palermo on July 12, 1633.

Arsenic was a popular poison because it doesn't have an odor or taste, so its presence in food or drink was hard to detect. Doctors couldn't find evidence of it in a poisoned corpse. Accused murderers who had used arsenic for their crimes usually went free because forensic scientists had no way of proving that arsenic was the poison of choice. That changed in 1836 when London chemist James Marsh developed a quick and easy test, the Marsh test, to detect arsenic in the body.

Because of Marsh's work, reliable tests for detecting arsenic are widely available. Arsenic breaks down very slowly. It can be detected in the body decades later. It also slows down the natural decomposition of human tissues, which makes it even easier for lab technicians to detect. Arsenic is so good at preserving bodies that it has been used to embalm them. For example, Elmer McCurdy, a nineteenth-century outlaw, was so well embalmed with arsenic that his body was shown in carnival sideshows for many decades after his death.

In 1840, shortly after James Marsh developed his arsenic test, Frenchwoman Marie Lafarge was tried for the murder of her husband, Charles Lafarge. She allegedly poisoned him with rat poison containing arsenic. Poison was in a Christmas cake she sent to him in Paris from their home in Le Glandier, France. He became sick, and doctors diagnosed him with cholera and sent him home to his wife. Despite bed rest and medication (doctors had prescribed eggnog), he got sicker and sicker. The family and servants eventually became suspicious when they observed Marie Lafarge adding a white powder to the eggnog for her husband. But it was too late to save him, and he died soon after. The family turned over the poisoned eggnog to the police. The authorities arrested Lafarge and charged her with murder.

Journalists covered the trial in daily newspapers in France. People from all over Europe came to Paris to see the trial. It became famous as one of the first trials to grab public attention through media coverage. It was also the first case to rely on forensic toxicological evidence. The Marsh test, central to the prosecutor's case, proved that the eggnog and Charles Lafarge's body contained arsenic. The court found Marie Lafarge guilty and sentenced her to life in prison. During her imprisonment, she wrote her memoirs, published in 1841. She was released in 1852, due to tuberculosis, and died later that year.

Queen Victoria ruled Britain at this time. Her long reign (1837–1901) was called the Victorian era. Victorian fashions for women focused on an exaggerated look through tight corsets, wide hoop skirts, and bustles under the skirt at the back. Green was a fashionable and desirable color in the Victorian era. The brightest, richest green dyes available in the Victorian era were Scheele's green and Paris green. The two dyes owed their green color to their main component—copper arsenite. The greens were used in many items, including dresses, gloves, silk flowers, wallpaper, and candles. Arsenic was everywhere in Victorian England. The arsenic didn't affect the affluent women wearing the green gowns with silk flowers. But it poisoned seamstresses, wallpaper installers, and dyers who worked closely with the dyes. They got warts, tumors, and cancers.

Pale white skin was also in fashion during the Victorian era, as a sign of wealth among upper-class women. It proved that wealthy women didn't have to work. They didn't have to labor in fields.

ARSENIC IN POP CULTURE, THE ARTS—AND ZOMBIES!

Arsenic is one of the oldest and most notorious poisons. It has proven to be irresistible to authors and screenwriters as a poison for unscrupulous characters wanting to get rid of rivals, spouses, or enemies. For example, French writer Gustave Flaubert wrote a famous novel in 1856 called *Madame Bovary*. It has been adapted to film three times—in 1949, 1991, and 2014. Emma Bovary commits suicide by swallowing arsenic. Flaubert describes in detail her slow, gruesome death. The popular 1944 film *Arsenic and Old Lace* is a dark comedy based on the 1939 play of the same name. In the film, directed by Frank Capra, star actor Cary Grant plays Mortimer Brewster. He discovers that his aunts have a very bad habit of poisoning lonely old bachelors with arsenic.

The best-known arsenic mysteries are Agatha Christie's, especially *The 4:50 from Paddington*, published in 1957. Films, plays, and even a game have been adapted from the book. Roald Dahl's short horror story *The Landlady*, from 1959, includes an arsenic appearance too.

Deborah Blum is the author of the 2010 nonfiction title *The Poisoner's Handbook: Murder and the Birth of Forensic Medicine in Jazz Age New York*. She feels that no one has ever written a more twisted arsenic murder mystery than Dorothy Sayers in *Strong Poison* (1930). Blum also has a very interesting theory about the origin of the legend of zombies. As a poison, arsenic not only kills its human victim, but it also kills the bacteria that break down the corpse. But if a body doesn't fully decompose, mold will grow on its face and the skin will turn green. Blum thinks unearthed victims of arsenic poisoning looked undead and could have been the origin of zombie legends.

Superstar Cary Grant (*third from right*) starred in the popular 1944 film *Arsenic and Old Lace*.

And they were not exposed to the sun. To protect their skin from the sun, they wore hats and gloves and carried umbrellas. They also bought a cream made of white arsenic (As_2O_3) mixed with chalk and vinegar. Massaged into the skin of the face and neck, the cream slowly destroyed red blood cells and made white skin paler.

ARSENIC TOXICOLOGY

The chemical symbol for arsenic is As. It has atomic number 33. That means it has thirty-three electrons and thirty-three protons. Its most commonly found form has forty-two neutrons in the nucleus. Arsenic is a metalloid—it has some metallic as well as nonmetallic properties. Arsenic makes up only about 0.00015 percent of Earth's crust and is the fifty-third most abundant element. The word *arsenic* comes from the ancient Syriac word *(al) zarniqa*, which means "yellow." The word originally described arsenic sulfide, which is yellow. The ancient Greeks called the mineral *arsenikon*, and the ancient Romans called it *arsenicum*.

Arsenic and its compounds are very toxic. Scientists talk about the toxicity of a compound in terms of its lethal dose 50 (LD_{50}). This is the amount of material that would kill 50 percent of an average population to have ingested (eaten or drunk) the material. The dose is normally measured in micrograms or milligrams of material per kilogram of test animal body weight. For example, the LD_{50} of white arsenic for rats is 15 mg per kg. That means that 0.015 g of white arsenic will kill half a population of rats weighing 1 kg each. If each rat weighs 2 kg, then 0.030 g would do the job. The lower the LD_{50}, the more toxic the material. Not all arsenic compounds are toxic, however. For example, arsenobetaine, with a LD_{50} of greater than 10,000 mg per kg, is less toxic than everyday table salt.

Toxicologists and medical professionals use the term *acute exposure* if a person has been poisoned or has been exposed to poison for a short time. Acute exposure is sometimes accidental.

Chronic exposure is the opposite. It is a long-term exposure, often to much lower concentrations of a toxic compound. Acute and chronic exposures have different symptoms. Symptoms for acute arsenic poisoning are headaches, confusion, diarrhea, blood in the urine, and vomiting. These symptoms can be mistaken for cholera, and in many parts of the world, cholera is still common. Chronic exposure typically comes from drinking or working with polluted well water and is one of the world's greatest environmental health hazards. Chronic exposure can lead to thickened skin and specific types of cancer, such as bladder, skin, and lung cancers. It can also lead to diabetes and cardiovascular (heart) diseases.

ARSENIC IN THE WATER

More than 40 million people in Bangladesh—or about 25 percent of its population of 163 million people—are at risk from arsenic-contaminated drinking water. This crisis dates back to the 1990s, when researchers first discovered arsenic in the nation's drinking water. The crisis is critical. Arsenic-related deaths in Bangladesh reach as many as forty-three thousand per year. The World Health Organization is a global institution that strives to combat diseases and build healthier futures for people all over the world. The organization has described the arsenic poisoning in Bangladesh as the "largest mass poisoning of a population in history."

Before the 1970s, most Bangladeshi villages obtained their water from shallow wells, standing water, and local ponds. Pathogens (bacteria, viruses, and microorganisms that cause diseases) severely contaminated them. Drinking the polluted water led to regular outbreaks of cholera and dysentery. Infant mortality was among the highest in the world, with a rate of 150 deaths per 1,000 live births. The United Nations Children's Fund works to help women and children in poor developing countries. The program partnered with the World Bank, an international financial institution that works to reduce global poverty, to solve the water problem in Bangladesh. Together, they oversaw and paid for eight million new wells. Workers drilled the wells 150 feet (46 m) deep, where the underground aquifers (pools of water) don't contain the cholera and dysentery pathogens commonly found in shallower water.

At first, the program seemed to be a great success. Infant mortality and diarrheal diseases decreased by more than 50 percent. But in the early 1990s, doctors reported the first cases of arsenic poisoning. Researchers soon linked the poisoning to the new wells. Drilling down to 150 feet (46 m) had not been a good idea after all because the sedimentary rocks at this depth are rich in arsenic. Rivers create this type of rock over thousands of years

with layer after layer of sediment and other rocky materials. When the wells were drilled, no one knew that arsenic is in the rocks, so no one tested for it. The arsenic dissolved in the well water. Because arsenic has no taste, color, or smell, no one noticed that the water was contaminated. It was only when people started having skin lesions and cancers of the bladder, skin, and kidneys that the Bangladeshi government realized they had an arsenic problem.

The only way to find contaminated wells is to test for arsenic, which is expensive. The Bangladeshi government, nongovernmental environmental and health organizations, and international donors have spent hundreds of millions of dollars to identify and replace contaminated wells. Yet the latest

A young boy in Bangladesh showed a photographer the skin lesions on his hand and legs from arsenic-contaminated water. Arsenic poisoning from contaminated well water leads to various cancers that still kill thousands of Bangladeshis every year.

estimates suggest that thousands of Bangladeshis are still dying from arsenic poisoning each year. The arsenic has also made its way into the food chain, mainly through rice grown in arsenic-rich standing water. The problem isn't only in Bangladesh either. India, Vietnam, China, and Cambodia also lie on formations of similar arsenic-rich rocks. Citizens in these nations are becoming dangerously ill from drinking and farming with arsenic-contaminated water.

FINDING SOLUTIONS FOR ARSENIC

The solution to the groundwater problem in Bangladesh is, first, to test all the wells for arsenic. For wells that test positive, workers either remove all the arsenic from the water once it comes out of the well or close the wells altogether. The most effective and easiest way to remove arsenic from water is to use a filter system. In Bangladesh the most commonly used filter system is the Sono arsenic filter system. Each filter costs between thirty-five and forty dollars to manufacture. The filters should be replaced every five years. Each is able to remove more than 98 percent of all arsenic. The filters also remove bacterial impurities from 5 to 8 gallons (20 to 30 L)

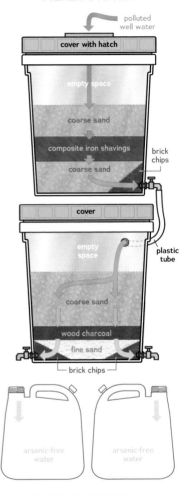

SONO ARSENIC FILTER SYSTEM

polluted well water

cover with hatch

empty space

coarse sand

composite iron shavings

brick chips

coarse sand

cover

empty space

plastic tube

coarse sand

wood charcoal

fine sand

brick chips

arsenic-free water

arsenic-free water

This effective Sono filtration system costs between thirty-five to forty dollars and removes more than 98 percent of all arsenic as well as bacterial impurities from the water. It can clean 5 to 8 gallons (20 to 30 L) of water a day.

of water a day, enough drinking water for about sixty people.

George Mason University chemistry professor Abul Hussam invented the system in 2006. It is a simple design with two buckets. The buckets are stacked on top of each other and placed next to the well. The top bucket contains coarse sand and thin pieces of iron, called iron shavings, or iron turnings. Well users pour water into the top bucket, and the sand slows the flow of water so the iron can bind to and capture the arsenic. As the water flows into the bottom bucket, the fine sand, wood charcoal, and brick chips in that bucket absorb and remove other contaminants and fine particles from the water. More than 280,000 Sono filters are in use in Bangladesh and neighboring countries.

One drawback to solutions is the cost of arsenic tests. It is so high that many households in Bangladesh can't afford to test. So they don't know whether their Sono filters have successfully removed the arsenic. An alternative to the filters is to drill wells at least 500 feet (150 m) deep. At that depth, experts know aquifers have enough arsenic-free groundwater to provide drinking water for Bangladesh for at least one thousand years. However, if too much water is removed from the deeper aquifers, arsenic-contaminated water from the shallower aquifers will be naturally sucked into those deeper aquifers. This may be a danger if farmers in Bangladesh continue to draw large amounts of water from deep aquifers.

WHAT CAN YOU DO?

The maximum contaminant level is a measure of the legal limit of a polluting substance in drinking water. In the United States, the EPA has set the level for arsenic to 0.010 mg arsenic in 1 L of water. This corresponds to ten arsenic atoms dissolved in ten billion water molecules. If you get your drinking water from a public water supply, your water is tested. It doesn't contain harmful amounts of arsenic. The United States Geological Survey publishes maps on the internet that show the concentration of arsenic in groundwater all over the United States. If you get your drinking water from a well, you can find out from the survey's site if the groundwater in your area has arsenic concentrations above ten parts per billion (ppb). If it does, have your well water tested for arsenic by a certified water-testing laboratory. It will cost about twenty to thirty dollars.

DR. ABUL HUSSAM AND THE SONO FILTER

Abul Hussam was born in Bangladesh in 1952. He left his homeland in 1978 to earn his PhD in chemistry at the University of Pittsburgh in Pennsylvania. After completing his studies, he stayed in the United States and became a professor in the Chemistry Department at George Mason University in Fairfax, Virginia. In 1993 he heard about the arsenic-contaminated drinking water in Bangladesh and started working on an inexpensive way to purify the water. He wanted a method that didn't require electricity. More than a decade later, with the help of his brothers (a physician and a businessperson), he invented the practical and inexpensive Sono filter system.

In 2007 the National Academy of Engineering—based in Washington, DC—awarded him the prestigious million-dollar Grainger Challenge Prize for Sustainability. He pledged to use $700,000 of the award money to build Sono filters for people who can't afford the filter and $250,000 for research into improving methods to remove arsenic from drinking water and to give the remaining $50,000 to George Mason University.

Dr. Abul Hussam, a chemistry professor, invented an inexpensive, easy-to-use water filter to deal with the arsenic problem in his homeland of Bangladesh.

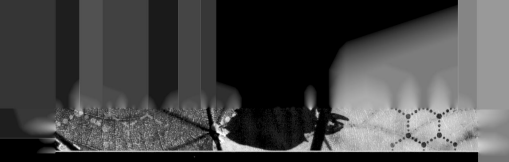

I n 1958 Rachel Carson's friend Olga Owens Huckins gave her
a copy of a letter she had sent to the *Boston Herald,* which
published it. Huckins described how the birds on her property
were dying after the State of Massachusetts had sprayed
the pesticide dichloro-diphenyl-trichloroethane (DDT) to kill
mosquitoes. Carson, a scientist and science writer, was intrigued.
She started investigating the effects on the environment and on
animals of large-scale pesticide applications. She interviewed
scientists and examined hundreds of cases in which pesticide
exposure had led to human health problems and ecological
damage. In 1962, after four years of research, Carson's findings

Famous photographer Alfred Eisenstaedt took this photo of biologist and
writer Rachel Carson with her microscope at her home in 1962. *Silent
Spring,* her groundbreaking book about the dangers of the chemical
pesticide DDT, came out that year.

were published as a book, *Silent Spring*. The title was inspired by an 1819 ballad by English poet John Keats. In the first verse of the ballad, called "La Belle Dame sans Merci" (The Beautiful Woman without Mercy), the poet writes, "The sedge has wither'd from the lake,/And no birds sing." The lines hint at a time when birdsong would no longer mark the start of spring.

Silent Spring pointed to synthetic pesticides as a dangerous way to control nature through chemistry. Pesticides are substances that people use to kill or control harmful insects, small animals, wild plants, and other unwanted organisms (pests). The book discussed the overuse and unintended ecological consequences of DDT and other persistent pesticides—those that do not decompose and bioaccumulate. It grabbed the public's attention. In *Silent Spring*, Carson showed that the biomagnification of DDT throughout the food chain—from small fish to bigger fish and from them to birds of prey that regularly feed on the big fish—had unforeseen and harmful consequences. For example, female birds exposed to high concentrations of DDT laid eggs whose shells were so thin they could not support the weight of the mother sitting on the eggs. The number of hatchlings decreased. In time, scientists saw a steep decline in populations of birds of prey, especially osprey in the northeastern United States.

Introduced during World War II, DDT was used to control insect-borne diseases such as malaria and typhus. By the early 1960s, scientists knew of the link between biomagnification of synthetic pesticides such as DDT and environmental harm. So the US Department of Agriculture, which then regulated pesticides, began to limit the use of DDT. Rachel Carson was the first person to gather all the information and present it in a way that caught the attention of the public. Since its publication, *Silent Spring* has sold two million copies. Carson's book and her campaign against synthetic pesticides, which she called biocides because they kill living things, launched the environmental movement of the late twentieth century. Senator Ernest Gruening, a Democrat from Alaska, told Carson that "every once in a while in the history of

BIOMAGNIFICATION

Persistent organic pesticides such as DDT dissolve better in fatty tissues than in water. So when contaminated water with these pesticides passes over a fish's gills, the pesticide chemicals will spread into the fish's fatty tissue and concentrate there. As the fish gets older, it will have more of these pesticides in the fatty tissues. This is called bioconcentration.

Over its lifetime, a big fish will eat many smaller fishes that also have bioconcentrated persistent organic pesticides in their fatty tissues. Along comes a large bird of prey. When it eats a big fish, it inherits all these pesticides the fish has accumulated in its lifetime. As illustrated in the infographic below, the concentration of these pesticides increases dramatically as they go up the food chain to bigger animals. This increase in concentration is called biomagnification. Because these pesticides tend to be very stable and do not dissolve in water, they remain in the food chain for decades. Our human exposure to them is through our food supply and not in the water we drink. Edible fish, especially freshwater fish such as carp, are the most likely source of these pesticides in humans.

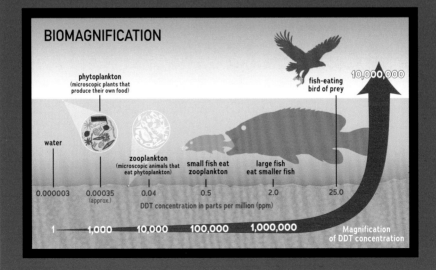

mankind, a book has appeared which has substantially altered the course of history." *Silent Spring* was one of those books.

For example, nine months after *Silent Spring* was published, the presidential Science Advisory Committee responded to President John F. Kennedy's request to examine the book's stark conclusions. The committee published a report on the use of pesticides. Its findings confirmed that bioaccumulation of pesticides is dangerous to human health and the environment, particularly to birds and fishes. The committee recommended the phaseout of persistent toxic pesticides. Carson died from breast cancer in 1964 and never got to see the formation of the EPA in 1970. In 1972 the EPA banned the agricultural use of DDT in the United States.

Since then bald eagles have made a comeback around the Great Lakes. The Arctic peregrine falcon is no longer on the list as an endangered species under the Endangered Species Conservation Act. Osprey are again common in New England.

FUMIGATING THE HALLS

About ten thousand years ago, our earliest ancestors first settled in permanent communities and started planting crops. They began to look for ways to control insect pests. Records from as early as 2500 BCE say that Sumerians (in present-day Iraq) rubbed foul-smelling sulfur compounds all over their bodies to repel pests. The Ebers Papyrus, an ancient Egyptian medical document from 1550 BCE, also describes the use of pesticides and other poisons. Around 1000 BCE, the Greek poet Homer wrote *The Odyssey*. In this Western classic, the hero Odysseus says, "Bring me brimstone and a brazier—medicinal fumes to purify my hall." Then the Chinese were using mercury and arsenic compounds to control body lice.

Three thousand years later, in 1880, the first mechanical pesticide sprayers allowed farmers to apply pesticides across large areas. At the time, lead arsenate (a highly toxic combination)

DDT: FALLING TO THE FLOOR

Swiss chemist Paul Hermann Müller (1899–1965) won the 1948 Nobel Prize in Physiology or Medicine for his development of DDT and its use in controlling the spread of insect-borne diseases.

In 1935 chemist Paul Müller was working for J. R. Geigy, a large chemical company in Switzerland. He was tasked with finding an insecticide that "would have a quick and powerful toxic effect upon the largest possible number of insect species while causing little or no harm to plants and warm-blooded animals." The pesticide should also be cheap to manufacture, insoluble in water, and have a long-lasting effect.

In four years, Müller tested 349 compounds before he tested DDT. He sprayed a solution of DDT onto the walls of a fly cage, let it dry, and released a housefly into the cage. It died. Further testing showed that DDT was a very efficient insecticide. According to Müller, "My fly cage was so toxic after a short period that even after very thorough cleaning of the cage, untreated flies, on touching the walls, fell to the floor. I could carry on my trials only after dismantling the cage, having it thoroughly cleaned and after that leaving it for about one month in the open air." Further tests revealed that DDT was tremendously effective against a wide range of insects, such as disease-carrying mosquitoes (malaria), lice (typhoid), and fleas (the plague).

was a cheap and commonly used pesticide. The first use of small airplanes to spray pesticides (lead arsenate dust) on croplands was in 1921. The planes, known as crop dusters, sprayed the chemical over fields in Ohio to control sphinx moth caterpillars, which attack tall trees.

Most modern pesticides are synthetic organic compounds. Organic compounds are made of molecules that have carbon atoms that form a central ring or chainlike structure. Modern pesticides break down quickly. They target only certain pests, while being less toxic to mammals.

In 1940 Geigy started making and selling DDT as both a spray and a powder. During World War II, US and allied armies used DDT to control the spread of malaria and typhoid. The pesticide was so effective that Müller was awarded the Nobel Prize in Physiology or Medicine in 1948 "for his discovery of the high efficiency of DDT as a contact poison against several arthropods [insects and other animals without skeletons]." In presenting the award, Professor G. Fisher praised DDT, saying "At [proper] insecticidal dosages it is practically non-toxic to humans, and acts in very small dosages on a large number of various species of insect. Furthermore, it is cheap, easily manufactured and exceedingly stable. A surface treated with DDT maintains its insecticidal properties for a long time, up to several months." Fisher also said that DDT had prevented many disease outbreaks. DDT completely eradicated malaria-carrying mosquitoes from the United States and Europe.

Between 1945 and 1972, more than 1.35 billion pounds (612 million kg) of DDT was used in the United States, mostly in agriculture and forestry. Had DDT been used to control only disease-carrying insects, large-scale problems would not have occurred. However, the excessive agricultural use of DDT led to dangerously high concentrations in birds, especially birds of prey such as bald eagles and osprey. With the publication of Rachel Carson's *Silent Spring* in 1962, DDT came under intense scrutiny. Its devastating health effects on wildlife could not be ignored, and the EPA banned its use in 1972.

In the United States in the twenty-first century, chemical manufacturers produce 1.1 million tons (0.9 million t) of pesticides each year. In the United States, 50 percent of pesticides are for agriculture. The other 50 percent is for domestic and recreational uses such as on lawns, in swimming pools, and on golf courses. Worldwide, 85 percent of pesticides are used in agriculture. The high use of pesticides on farm fields has led to pesticide-contaminated food crops. In the United States, about half of all agricultural produce contains measurable amounts of at least one pesticide. Modern pesticides break down quickly.

POPS

In 2001 various nations negotiated a worldwide treaty—the Stockholm Convention on Persistent Organic Pollutants (POPs). The treaty went into effect in 2004. It has been signed by 180 nations and the European Union. The convention either fully bans or restricts DDT and other persistent organic pollutants. Nations that have signed the treaty but have not ratified (approved) it include the United States, Italy, Malaysia, and Israel.

The Stockholm Convention defines persistent organic pollutants as "chemical substances that persist in the environment, bioaccumulate through the food web, and pose a risk of causing adverse effects to human health and the environment." Pesticides, industrial solvents, paints, and pharmaceutical by-products are all examples of these common pollutants. Because they evaporate easily, they spread in the air and winds blow them all over the world. They generally don't break down in the environment, so people don't have to reapply them often. They are also water insoluble so that they aren't washed away. Yet they bioaccumulate and cause health risks to predators such as humans that are higher on the food chain. These pollutants have not been released in the polar regions, yet they have even been found in the fatty tissues of polar bears.

Polar bears eat mostly fatty ringed seals, which pass high concentrations of POPs up the food chain to the top predators. Scientists from nations with polar bears have been monitoring bear tissues for decades to learn more about the concentration of POPs in the Arctic animals.

The health concerns from pesticides are greatest for agricultural workers, who apply the chemicals and harvest the crops. Workers are more likely to suffer from cancer, neurological disease, and reproductive problems.

FINDING PESTICIDE SOLUTIONS

The United States, Canada, and most of Europe banned the use of DDT in the mid-1970s. However, US and Canadian chemical companies continued to manufacture DDT to sell in other parts of the world, particularly Africa. The Stockholm Convention on Persistent Organic Pollutants, which went into effect in 2004, stopped the

Before DDT was banned in the United States, magazines regularly ran ads for DDT products, claiming they were safe. This ad from Penn Salt Chemicals appeared in *Time* magazine in June 1947.

agricultural use of DDT around the globe. However, DDT is still the most effective pesticide for killing malaria-carrying mosquitoes. These insects are widespread in many parts of Africa, South America, and Asia, killing about five hundred thousand people every year. So the pesticide still is used legally to control malaria-bearing mosquitoes in those areas.

Biomagnification is one of the major consequences of DDT spraying. To prevent biomagnification with other pesticides, chemists have developed compounds that dissolve in water and break down within a few days or weeks. This has been a very

HOUSEHOLD PESTICIDES

About 80 to 90 percent of US households contain at least one synthetic pesticide. They include products such as flea powders for pets, weed killers for the garden, and ant traps. This table provides a simple overview of common types of pesticides and the living things they target. They are all toxic and should be handled carefully, according to directions.

PESTICIDE TYPE	TARGET ORGANISM
Algicide	Algae
Bactericide	Bacteria
Disinfectant	Microorganisms
Herbicide	Plants
Insecticide	Insects
Rodenticide	Rodents

effective development. Improved pesticides do not biomagnify up the food chain, although they tend to have more acute (short-term) toxicity. They are more dangerous to the people who make and apply the pesticides.

SPECIES-SPECIFIC INSECTICIDES

Pesticides that are used to control insects are called insecticides. The perfect insecticides are absorbed only by one species and therefore only affect one species. Chemists are always searching for new insecticides that target a particular pest without damaging the rest of an environment. One example of an effective species-specific chemical is hexaflumuron. Insecticide manufacturers use it in products that target termites. These insects are a big problem in the United States, where they infest 1.5 million houses each year. Termites eat wood, and the infestations result in about $1.5 billion in damages.

Hexaflumuron-based products are species-specific synthetic pesticides. Manufacturers infuse wood bait with the chemical. Then they place the bait in a serrated (notched) plastic tube. The whole setup is called the Sentricon System. Termites live underground, so exterminators place several tubes in the ground near an infested home. Very few insects besides termites are interested in or can get to the wood bait. Even if they could get to the bait, the hexaflumuron is an antimolting agent. It is only harmful to termites and other insects that molt, or shed their outer shells or skin. Molting is part of metamorphosis, a series of life stages in insect development. Termites that are attracted to the bait stations will eat some of the hexaflumuron and bring it back to their termite colony. The chemical spreads throughout the colony, killing all the termites. Very little insecticide is needed to kill large numbers of termites, and the termites do most of the work of distributing the insecticide. The insecticide is termite specific and does not harm ladybugs and other beneficial insects.

Hexaflumuron is much less harmful than traditional termite pesticides. In 1994, one year before the Sentricon System was commercially released, the EPA classified it as the first-ever reduced-risk pesticide. In 2000 the EPA awarded its manufacturer—Dow AgroSciences—the Presidential Green Chemistry Challenge award for the product. The EPA gives this award every year to recognize chemical technologies whose manufacture and application have minimal impact on the environment. In 2018 the Sentricon System is still one of the most commonly used forms of termite pest control.

The most recent Presidential Green Chemistry Challenge award to go to a pesticide company was in 2010. (The award goes to other industries too.) That year the Illinois-based company Clarke won the award for a larvicide (a product that kills larvae) called Natular. The Natular system is a very clever way of using

LIFE CYCLE OF A LADYBUG

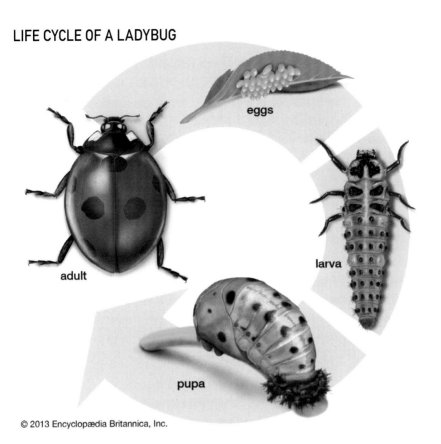

eggs

larva

pupa

adult

This infographic shows the life stages that are part of the metamorphosis of a ladybug, from egg to adult.

the chemical compound spinosad to kill mosquito larvae, which live in standing water. Spinosad does not normally work in water, but Clarke developed a system that does. A capsule slowly releases spinosad into water over a long time—180 days—so the larvicide does its job. The Natular system won the award because it is less toxic, less persistent in the environment, and cleaner to make than all competing larvicides.

STERILE INSECT TECHNIQUE

In some insect species, such as cotton pest moths, screwworms (also called blowflies), and Mediterranean fruit flies, the females only mate once. An effective method for controlling the insect populations in those species is the sterile insect technique. This technique has been around since the mid-1950s. Lab technicians raise large numbers of a specific insect and mark the male larvae with dye. When the insects are in their adult stage, technicians radiate the males. Radiation sterilizes the males, which technicians then release back into the wild. When a female mates with that male, he cannot fertilize the eggs that would otherwise become the next generation of offspring.

Like other insects, the screwworm goes through metamorphosis. The female adult feeds on fluids from warm-blooded host animals. She will lay between one hundred and four hundred eggs in open wounds or in mouth, anal, or nose areas of the host animals. In these places, the larvae will have the nutrition, warmth, and moisture they need to grow. When they hatch, the larvae burrow their way into the host, eating the surrounding flesh. The first signs of a screwworm infestation are a reddish-brown discharge that leaks from the host animal. The discharge sometimes smells unpleasant. After five to seven days of feasting on the host's flesh, the larvae eject themselves from the flesh and drop to the ground. There they become pupae and eventually adults.

For many decades, livestock farmers were looking for a solution to the screwworm problem. In 1959 the screwworm in Florida became the first species that scientists successfully controlled with the sterile insect technique. The method was so effective that it eliminated the insect from the United States in 1966 and Mexico in 1991. The technique also eliminated screwworms in most of Central America. Screwworms are still a major problem in equatorial

Africa and Southeast Asia. One of the largest known screwworm outbreaks in the world occurred in 1989, affecting more than 2.7 million sheep in northern Africa. To respond to the crisis, a facility in Mexico produced 1.26 billion sterilized male screwworms. Released from planes over the site of the infestation, the sterilized insects successfully controlled the outbreak.

Around the world every month, trucks and planes release more than one billion sterilized insects to control a large variety of pests. For example, workers release hundreds of millions of sterilized male screwworms and Mediterranean fruit flies every year in places such as South Africa, Spain, and Australia. Unlike the female insects, the males can mate more than once and will spend

A worker loads sterilized male screwworms onto an airplane. The plane will drop the insects over targeted areas in Texas to control the pests and the damage they would otherwise do to livestock there.

their lives looking for females. With the release of large numbers of sterile males, scientists can exterminate (collapse) the local population of a pest.

GENETICALLY MODIFIED ORGANISMS

Mosquitoes live in many different climates, including the Arctic. According to some estimates, the United States alone is home to about forty thousand mosquitoes per person. That's about thirteen trillion mosquitoes! They are the deadliest animals in the world. They are vectors for (carry) many deadly diseases such as malaria, dengue fever, Zika, and yellow fever.

Only pregnant female mosquitoes bite their victims. They live on blood to nurture the eggs they are carrying. Female mosquitoes that are not pregnant and male mosquitoes live from eating nectar and pollen. Pregnant females spread mosquito-borne diseases during their blood meals. Mosquitoes infect more than seven hundred million people annually, and at least two million people die from these infections every year.

According to the Stockholm Convention, DDT only can be used to combat malaria-carrying *Anopheles* mosquitoes. A house sprayed with DDT will stay mosquito-free for more than six months. No other ways of controlling these mosquitoes that are anywhere as effective as DDT are yet available. The sterile insect technique hasn't worked with mosquitoes so far because radiated, sterile male mosquitoes are physically weak. Female mosquitoes aren't attracted to them. Instead, they choose nonsterile male mosquitoes for mating.

Aedes aegypti mosquitoes transmit dengue, Zika, and yellow fever. A small English biotech company, Oxitec, has genetically modified these mosquitoes so that they produce offspring that don't progress beyond the larval stage. Genetic modification (GM) involves the change, addition, or removal of genetic material (deoxyribonucleic acid, or DNA) of an organism. The modification of genes changes a creature's characteristics. For example, GM *A. aegypti* mosquitoes only live for a week and their offspring die before they reach adulthood. So the GM mosquitoes don't persist in the environment. The World Health Organization recommends GM mosquitoes as an environmentally friendly method for combating *A. aegypti* mosquitoes to prevent Zika outbreaks. An extensive US Food and Drug Administration study from 2017 concluded that a trial release of the Oxitec mosquitoes would be safe for the environment and for people. The mosquitoes are being released in Malaysia, Panama, and Brazil.

In the small city of Piracicaba, northwest of São Paulo, Brazil, Oxitec has a facility that can produce sixty million GM male *A. aegypti* mosquitoes per week. Dengue fever has been a crisis in São Paulo, where almost half a million people a year (in a population of more than twelve million) come down with the disease. By regularly releasing GM male mosquitoes in Piracicaba, the city has seen a 90 percent decrease in dengue fever cases there since 2015. At its home base in England, Oxitec can generate one billion GM mosquito eggs per week. The eggs are shipped to various locations across the globe, where they are reared and released as needed. GM and the sterile insect technique are two of the most promising high-tech methods for finding green, species-specific solutions for pest control around the world.

WHAT CAN YOU DO?

Mosquitoes need water to reproduce. The best way to combat mosquitoes is to remove sources of still, unmoving water where the insects can breed. Make sure to change the water in birdbaths regularly. Or think about removing birdbaths from your garden altogether. If the gutters in your family's house have standing water, ask an adult to clean them out.

Mosquito nets are an affordable and effective way to prevent being bitten by mosquitoes at night. You can contribute to the United Nations Foundation's Nothing But Nets campaign to help protect families from mosquito-borne illnesses. Go to https://nothingbutnets.net/ to learn more.

About 40 percent of the world's population is at risk of dengue fever infection—the most common mosquito-borne disease. *A. aegypti,* the vector for dengue, thrives in urban areas. It is more at home in the city than in the jungle. *A. aegypti* prefers to lay its eggs in containers such as metal drums and earthenware jars. They also like plastic containers and abandoned car tires that collect rainwater. Make sure you have no containers of standing water in your garden, porch, deck, or lawn. Swimming pools with chlorine are okay because the chlorine kills the mosquito larvae. If you have a pond, add some fish. They will eat the mosquito eggs and larvae.

To prevent the spread of dengue fever in Singapore during mosquito season, a homeowner can be fined for having mosquito-breeding sites, such as a glass of water, in the garden.

If you have removed all the standing water around your house and still have mosquitoes, try wearing lightweight long pants and long-sleeved shirts to protect yourself from bites. If you are sitting outside on a porch or stoop, set up a fan. It will blow the critters away from you.

Only use pest-control products if you have to. This may include a walk in the deep woods or a jungle vacation. It may also include infestations of disease-carrying animals inside the home. Professionals can help with that. When you use pesticides on your body, apply them carefully and as described in the directions. Using too much pesticide and too often is not as effective at killing pests as applying only the recommended dose.

Without photosynthesis, life on Earth as we know it would not exist. Photosynthesis is the process by which green plants convert water, carbon dioxide, and light energy from the sun into sugars. Plants break down the sugars to release chemical energy. The plants use about half the chemical energy in their daily lives. The other half remains stored in their bodies until they die. Then the energy very slowly converts to energy-rich fossil fuels.

Chinese workers commute as smoke billows from a coal-fired power plant in Shanxi. Heavy dependence on burning coal for energy has made China the source of nearly one-third of the world's total carbon dioxide emissions, the pollutant that is the primary cause of global warming and climate change. The United States is also a major contributor of CO_2, releasing more of the greenhouse gas per person than any other country in the world.

Photosynthesis directly and indirectly feeds all organisms on the planet. All the energy in the plants and animals we eat comes from the sun. For example, grains, fruits, and vegetables all get their energy from the sun. Cows, whose beef some people eat, do not themselves photosynthesize. But all their energy comes from the grass they eat, which in turn gets its life energy from the sun and photosynthesis.

When microorganisms, plants, and animals die, they sometimes become fossils. Fossilization happens under certain conditions (intense pressure and heat deep underground) and over millions of years. The fossilized material becomes coal, natural gas, and petroleum (oil). Known as fossil fuels, these naturally fossilized materials are hydrocarbons. They are composed mainly of carbon and hydrogen atoms. The more hydrogen atoms per carbon atom, the more energy and the less pollution a material will produce when

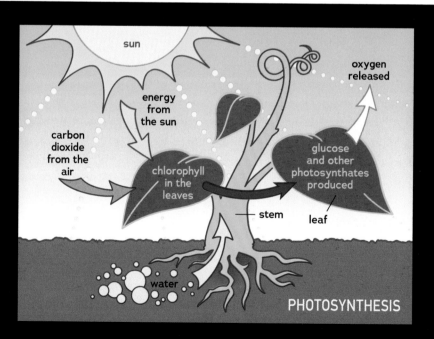

Photosynthesis is the process by which green plants use the sun's energy, carbon dioxide, and chlorophyll to produce the nutrients they need to survive.

burned. So fuels such as natural gas, with more hydrogen atoms per carbon atom, contain more energy and produce less pollution. Natural gas is the cleanest fossil fuel, with about four hydrogen atoms per carbon atom. But coal has a 1-to-1 ratio of hydrogen to carbon atoms, so it produces less energy and more pollution by comparison.

Fuel	H/C ratio	Energy content (kJ/g)	CO2 released (mol/10³kJ)
Hydrogen	—	120	—
Gas	4/1	51.6	1.2
Petroleum	2/1	43.6	1.6
Coal	1/1	39.3	2.0
Wood	1/10	14.9	3.4

In the United States, Americans burned wood as the main source of fuel before the Industrial Revolution. This period of technological innovation started in England in the 1830s. It soon spread to western Europe and the United States. Manufacturers began building factories in cities to produce large amounts of goods quickly and cheaply. Wood does not generate much energy, and with ten carbon atoms per hydrogen atom, it is highly polluting. So manufacturers turned instead to higher-energy coal to fuel their furnaces. Newly invented steam locomotives (trains) stoked their boilers with coal too. Coal provided the energy for the Industrial Revolution. This fossil fuel produces more than twice the energy of an equivalent mass of wood. However, coal is highly polluting too.

COAL
Coal is a solid formed from lignin, which exists naturally in land-based woody plants. After millions of years deep in the ground—under high pressures and high temperatures—the lignin changes

into coal. Areas of the world with rich deposits of coal include China, the United States, India, and Russia.

During its formation, coal absorbs surrounding elements such as sulfur dioxide, uranium, and heavy metals such as mercury and lead. When people burn coal, it releases large amounts of these pollutants along with fine particulate matter (PM), or soot. However, coal still is used in power plants because it is abundant. The United States, for example, has enough coal to last for more than two hundred years. Coal is also inexpensive to buy and easy to transport by train.

In coal-powered plants, coal is burned to heat water in boilers to generate steam. The steam is under pressure and is directed at turbine generators to turn their blades. The generators produce electricity for homes, businesses, and manufacturers. Power plants in the United States install filtration and scrubber systems in the smokestacks. As exhaust fumes pass through the smokestacks, the filters and scrubbers capture coal-based pollutants such as mercury, sulfur dioxide, and nitrogen dioxide. However, power plants do not remove the carbon dioxide emissions because plant managers cannot afford the expensive carbon dioxide scrubbers.

PARTICULATE MATTER

When organic, carbon-based materials burn, they can release particulate matter. PM is a mixture of solid particles and liquid droplets suspended in the air. Some of the particles, such as soot, smoke, and dust, are visible with the naked eye. Others are so fine they can be seen only with a microscope. Large volumes of fine PM often form a haze. It can hang over an area and limit visibility.

Solid particulate matter is often referred to as dust, or soot, and the liquid form of PM is mist and fog. Any collection of PM suspended in air is called an aerosol. The smaller the particles are, the longer they stay suspended in the air. Most of the fine particles come from the incomplete combustion (burning) of coal, oil, gasoline, and diesel fuel. In neighborhoods where people burn wood for heating, wood stoves are responsible for up to 80 percent of the fine PM suspended in the air during the winter months.

Breathing particulate matter is extremely hazardous to human and animal health. Toxic organic compounds and metals that are naturally in the combusted material stick on or dissolve in the particles. So when we breathe PM, we are also taking toxic compounds into our respiratory systems. Nose hairs and the throat catch the larger particles, which generally don't make it to the lungs. However, the finer particles do penetrate deeply into the lungs, where they can stick to cell surfaces and release their toxic payloads. Smaller PM is harder to remove with filters, so the air has

Large numbers of cars around the world add particulate matter to the air through burning gasoline to power their engines. PM is harmful to human health. This image is from Los Angeles, where almost 6.5 million cars crowd the roads.

a higher concentration of small particles than larger ones. Fine PM in the air is responsible for a greater negative impact on human health than any other gaseous pollutant. Since fine PM is the most damaging to health, most environmental regulations and studies focus on the fine particles. Research shows that both chronic (long term) and acute (short term) exposure to high concentrations of fine PM are linked to higher rates of death, from diseases such as lung cancer and asthma.

THE PM INDEX

Scientists use the PM index to measure the amount of particulate matter in the atmosphere. The index quantifies the mass (in micrograms) of particulate matter that is suspended in a given volume (in cubic meters) of air. Scientists measure the diameter (in micrometers) of the particles themselves. For example, all particles in a cubic meter of air with a diameter smaller than 10 micrometers (10µm) are measured in the PM_{10} index. Particles with a diameter smaller than 10 mm are inhalable particles because we breathe them into our lungs. Very fine particles with a diameter of less than 2.5 micrometers are measured in the $PM_{2.5}$ index. Scientists refer to $PM_{2.5}$ particles as respirable particles because they penetrate the deepest into our lungs. So they are the most toxic particles.

The World Health Organization cautions cities to avoid annual $PM_{2.5}$ indexes of higher than 10 µg/m³. In the United States, Los Angeles, California; New York City, Newark, New Jersey; and Philadelphia, Pennsylvania, all have annual $PM_{2.5}$ indexes just above 10 µg/m³. The worlds most polluted cities are in China, India, Iran, and Saudi Arabia. They have $PM_{2.5}$ way above 120 µg/m³. The high indexes in China and India are related to expanding and unregulated manufacturing. In Iran and Saudi Arabia, intense concentrations of oil extraction and refining contribute to the high $PM_{2.5}$ there.

NATURAL GAS

This fossil fuel is less polluting and more energy rich than coal. It is formed over millions of years as ancient marine organisms are naturally compressed under deep layers of buried sediment at very high temperatures and pressures. The fossil fuels that form in these conditions are liquids and gases. About 60 to 90 percent of natural gas is methane (CH_4). It contains sulfur compounds, especially hydrogen sulfide (H_2S), which pollutes the air when the gas is burned. Refineries process natural gas to remove these impurities before selling it.

As early as 500 BCE, people in China used natural gas as a fuel to boil seawater to make it safe to drink. This is called distillation. The Chinese piped the gas through the hollow interior of bamboo stalks to burners. In the twenty-first century, natural gas is a source of fuel mainly in North America and Europe for heating homes and other buildings. It also fuels stoves for cooking, and it fuels some cars and buses. Companies transport natural gas across vast distances through long steel pipelines. The gas is under high pressure, and some of the gas leaks, releasing significant amounts of methane into the atmosphere.

Areas with rich reserves of natural gas include Russia, Iran, Qatar, and the United States. The United States is the biggest producer of natural gas in the world. And 70 percent of all the natural gas produced in the United States is removed from the ground through fracking.

PETROLEUM

Petroleum, or crude oil, is a complex mixture of thousands of compounds, mainly hydrocarbons. The hydrocarbons range from methane (CH_4), with one carbon atom bound to four hydrogen atoms, to compounds with almost one hundred carbons. The word *petroleum* comes from the Greek words *petra* (rock) and *elion* (oil).

FRACKING

Some of Earth's deposits of natural gas and oil are easy to find and easy to mine. Others are very hard to reach. Some are very deep underground. Others are stuck in the rocks they were formed in and haven't moved to more easily accessible rocks. As we use up the easy-to-reach deposits, mining companies are looking for new technologies to get the hard-to-reach deposits. Mining companies use two technologies—horizontal drilling and hydraulic fracturing (or fracking)—together to reach these deposits.

Companies rely on horizontal drilling to reach deposits of natural gas and oil that are at least 5,000 feet (1,524 m) underground. Natural gas and oil are in layers of shale. Miners drill narrow shafts, or boreholes, to reach the shale. Then they turn the huge drill bit to run parallel, or horizontally, to Earth's surface for 1 or 2 miles (1.6 to 3.2 km). Engineers then set off a series of regularly spaced explosive charges along the boreholes to fracture, or crack, the shale. They force millions of gallons of hydraulic fluid into the cracks at pressures of 9,000 pounds per square inch (633 kg per sq. cm) or more. The hydraulic fluid contains mainly water, sand, and lubricating agents. The intense pressure of the fluid expands the cracks and forces the natural gas in the shale to flow up the boreholes to the surface. An average horizontally drilled well will use 6 million gallons (23 million L) of fracking fluid in its lifetime. (The lifetime of one of these wells is about seven or eight years.) The sand and lubricating agents in the fracking fluid keep the cracks open after most of the water is brought back to the surface so that the gas and oil will continue to flow.

ADVANTAGES OF FRACKING

Fracking allows mining companies to reach many more US deposits of oil and natural gas and to sell them to US power companies. Energy companies don't have to buy as much fuel from foreign companies to meet US demands. Most US politicians want US companies to buy as little from overseas companies as possible so that the United States can be energy independent.

DISADVANTAGES OF FRACKING

Fracking is dirty business. After a drilling, miners have to dispose of the millions of gallons of fracking fluid that comes back to the surface. That fluid is polluted with acids, salts, and lubricants. Diesel generators run around the clock to power a well's hydraulic machinery, releasing particulate matter and CO_2. Trucks that burn diesel fuel haul hydraulic fluid to the wells over long distances every day of the year.

They too release PM and CO_2 into the atmosphere. Methane leakage occurs at all stages of natural gas extraction and transport. Experts also suspect that fracking causes increases in seismic activity, which creates small earthquakes that may cause structural damage to local buildings. Fracking sometimes pollutes groundwater when the boreholes pass through groundwater aquifers and ooze lubricating fluids and natural gas into the groundwater. Fracking requires such large amounts of sand that companies are always looking for new places to mine more supplies of sand. They are paying farmers for the right to mine sand rather than grow crops on their land. This leaves many people concerned about using land for energy rather than for food to feed people.

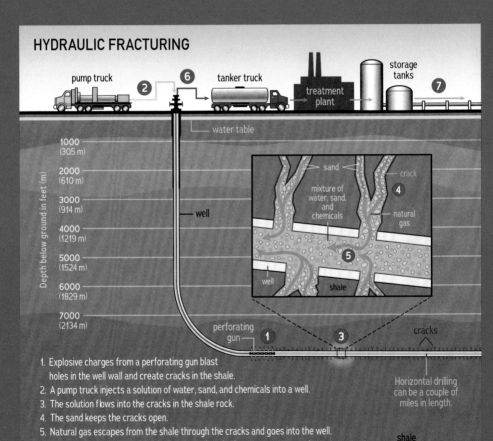

HYDRAULIC FRACTURING

pump truck
2
6
tanker truck
treatment plant
storage tanks
7

water table

Depth below ground in feet (m)

1000 (305 m)
2000 (610 m)
3000 (914 m)
4000 (1219 m)
5000 (1524 m)
6000 (1829 m)
7000 (2134 m)

well

sand
mixture of water, sand, and chemicals
crack
4
natural gas
5
well
shale

perforating gun
1
3
cracks

Horizontal drilling can be a couple of miles in length.

shale

1. Explosive charges from a perforating gun blast holes in the well wall and create cracks in the shale.
2. A pump truck injects a solution of water, sand, and chemicals into a well.
3. The solution flows into the cracks in the shale rock.
4. The sand keeps the cracks open.
5. Natural gas escapes from the shale through the cracks and goes into the well.
6. The gas is pumped out of the well, collected, and taken to a treatment plant.
7. After being treated, the natural gas is piped to homes and businesses.

Oil companies mine crude oil from rich seams of the fossil fuel deep underground and deep under the ocean floor. They extract about ninety-five million barrels of crude oil per day from oil wells all over the world. Saudi Arabia has the largest reserves of crude oil, with one-fifth of the world's oil. Other areas with plentiful deposits of oil include Venezuela, Canada, and Iran. After extracting oil from the ground, it goes to refineries where the crude oil is heated in distillation towers. They separate the oil into different fractions (portions) according to their boiling points. The most useful fraction as a fuel are the short crude oil hydrocarbons—those with one to four carbon atoms. They are gases at room temperature and include methane, ethane (C_2H_6), propane (C_3H_8), and butane (C_4H_{10}). These are the same gases as in natural gas, and they can be used just like natural gas.

About one-fifth of all extracted crude oil is hydrocarbons with five to twelve carbon atoms. They boil at low temperature and make gasoline for cars and trucks. The longer hydrocarbons—those with more than seventeen carbon atoms—boil at temperatures of more than 660°F (350°C). This fraction of crude oil is viscous. The shorter hydrocarbons in this fraction (twelve to twenty-one carbons) are used to produce diesel fuels. The longer ones are between a solid and a liquid state and are used as lubricating oils. Crude oil is also the source of wax and tar, and it contains the chemical building blocks of most plastic and pharmaceutical products.

Crude oil contains sulfur, and the sulfur is much easier to remove from liquid petroleum than from solid coal. So petroleum is a much cleaner fuel when it burns, releasing fewer pollutants than coal. Like coal, burning petroleum products in gasoline engines, industrial plants, or refineries produces fine particles that are harmful to human health.

Particulate matter from burning fossil fuels results in a health hazard we can see as dust or haze. Burning fossil fuels also releases carbon dioxide (CO_2), an invisible gas that is of even greater concern than PM.

THE GREENHOUSE EFFECT

In 1827 French mathematician Joseph Fourier proposed a radically new theory—the greenhouse effect. He suggested that gases in the atmosphere naturally trap heat on Earth just as a pane of glass in a greenhouse traps heat there. Other research has proven him right. Without atmospheric gases trapping the sun's infrared radiation in Earth's atmosphere, the average temperature of Earth would be -0.4°F (-18°C). All water would be frozen, and no life as we know it would be on Earth. Scientists have proven that the greenhouse effect warms Earth to an average of 59°F (15°C). Then a variety of life-forms can survive. Fourier was also one of the first scientists to point out that human activity will change the amount of thermal radiation (heat) trapped in the atmosphere, leading to climate change.

About sixty years after Fourier proposed the greenhouse effect, Swedish chemist Svante Arrehenius published "The Influence of Carbonic Acid (Carbon Dioxide) in the Air upon the Temperature of the Ground." The article described how carbon dioxide in the atmosphere traps Earth's heat. He also accurately calculated the temperature increases caused over time by the rise in carbon dioxide in the atmosphere. From these calculations, he concluded that a reduction of the amount of carbon dioxide in the air caused Earth's glacial periods, when thick sheets of ice covered large parts of the planet. By the twenty-first century, scientists agree that carbon dioxide and other greenhouse gases are increasing in concentration in Earth's atmosphere through human activities. As Fourier had predicted, the average temperature of Earth is increasing, beyond 59°F (15°C), and is leading to climate change.

LIGHT AND INFRARED SPECTROSCOPY

Light is a form of electromagnetic radiation, or energy. This radiation travels in waves, like waves on the ocean. The distance between the crest (top) of one electromagnetic wave and the crest of the next electromagnetic wave is a wavelength. The shorter the wavelength, the higher the energy of the radiation.

Human eyes can see only a small fraction of the electromagnetic spectrum (*facing page*), or range. This portion of the range is the visible spectrum. The colors in the visible spectrum range from red, with the longest wavelengths and the least energy, to orange, yellow, green, blue, and violet. Violet has the shortest, most energetic wavelengths. Just below red light is infrared radiation. It has less energy than visible light, and the human eye doesn't see it. However, when infrared light shines on our skin, we can feel our skin heat up. Mosquitoes, snakes, mantis shrimp, and some fishes can see infrared radiation. The sun emits mainly visible radiation and a little infrared and ultraviolet radiation, while Earth gives off infrared radiation.

Molecules at room temperature continuously vibrate. A molecule will absorb light when its energy and its wavelength match one of the molecule's internal vibrations. Molecules with three or more atoms normally have some vibrations that absorb infrared light. The molecules of the most common gases in the atmosphere—nitrogen (N_2), oxygen (O_2), and argon (Ar)—are composed of fewer than three atoms each. So they do not absorb infrared radiation. The molecules of water (H_2O), carbon dioxide (CO_2), and methane (CH_4) all have three or more atoms. Their vibrations match the energies of specific wavelengths of infrared radiation and will absorb that radiation and trap heat.

CO_2

Carbon dioxide and other gases that absorb the infrared radiation released by the sun and Earth are greenhouse gases. The increasing concentration of these gases in the atmosphere, which then traps more heat, causes climate change. Greenhouse gases concentrate in the atmosphere when the sources and amounts of gas emissions (mostly from factories and cars) are greater than their sinks. A *sink* is a process or organism that removes a greenhouse gas from the atmosphere. When the source and the sink are about equal, the concentration of a greenhouse gas will remain at equilibrium, or constant.

Spectroscopy is the study of the interaction between electromagnetic radiation and chemical compounds. Infrared spectroscopy mainly focuses on chemical compounds as they absorb and emit infrared radiation. Scientists use an infrared spectrometer to change the wavelength of a beam of infrared radiation that is sent through the sample. The device then records which wavelengths the substance absorbs. Spectroscopy shows, for example, that carbon dioxide's vibrations absorb infrared radiation. This is why high volumes of CO_2 in Earth's atmosphere are causing global warming and climate change and why nations are working to lower CO_2 emissions.

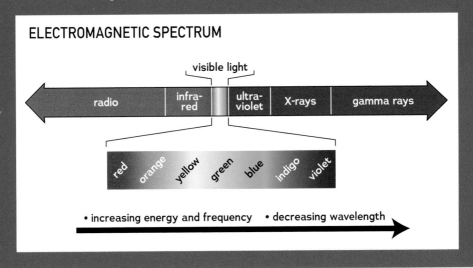

ELECTROMAGNETIC SPECTRUM

The three main sources of carbon dioxide in Earth's atmosphere are

- the burning of fossil fuels (combustion)
- trees and other living organisms that naturally exhale carbon dioxide (respiration) at least part of every day. Trees take in carbon dioxide and give off oxygen when they are photosynthesizing during the day. They give off carbon dioxide when they respire (breathe).
- concrete manufacturing in which limestone ($CaCO_3$) is heated to 18,000°F (10,000°C) to produce lime (CaO)

and carbon dioxide. The lime is a critical component of cement. Large amounts of carbon dioxide are released as a by-product of the process and in the combustion required to reach 18,000°F.

Combustion of fossil fuels and concrete production have both dramatically increased since the Industrial Revolution. Earth also has more people (more than seven billion) than ever before. We also have millions of cars, thousands of planes, and innumerable power plants and factories that all rely on burning fossil fuels. With growing populations and cities, humans are also constructing more and more buildings that require concrete.

Carbon dioxide has two natural sinks—green plants and natural bodies of water. Trees, plants, and forests use carbon dioxide as a key part of photosynthesis. Bodies of water naturally dissolve carbon dioxide. Yet we are removing a very large and important carbon dioxide sink as we burn rain forests to make way for cattle farms, rice paddies, and human habitation. And while the sources for carbon dioxide are increasing, the sinks are not. This means that the concentration of carbon dioxide is steadily increasing.

Scientists measure the concentration of carbon dioxide in the atmosphere in parts per million (ppm), or the number of CO_2 molecules in every million molecules of gas. In preindustrial times, the average world CO_2 levels were about 280 ppm. In 2016 the levels passed 400 ppm for the first time in four million years. That means that in every one million gas molecules in the atmosphere, at least four hundred are CO_2 molecules. Even the carbon dioxide levels at all the South Pole research stations have surpassed 400 ppm.

Most of the world's population lives in the Northern Hemisphere, so the greatest volume of carbon dioxide emissions comes from this part of the planet. Carbon dioxide emissions stay in the

Forests are natural sinks, which absorb greenhouse gases such as carbon dioxide from the atmosphere. With fewer natural sinks, greenhouse gases are increasing in Earth's atmosphere.

atmosphere for years because it takes time for the gas to dissolve in seawater and for trees and plants to absorb it. Meanwhile, air currents spread the CO_2 all over the world, so carbon emissions are a global problem. "The increase of carbon dioxide is everywhere . . . if you emit carbon dioxide in New York, some fraction of it will be in the South Pole next year," said Pieter Tans, a senior scientist with the National Oceanic and Atmospheric Administration's Earth System Research Laboratory in Boulder, Colorado.

METHANE

Methane is another greenhouse gas that impacts Earth. It is fifty times more effective at absorbing infrared radiation than the same mass of carbon dioxide. Yet methane currently causes only one-third the amount of global warming that carbon dioxide does because humans and animals produce less of it.

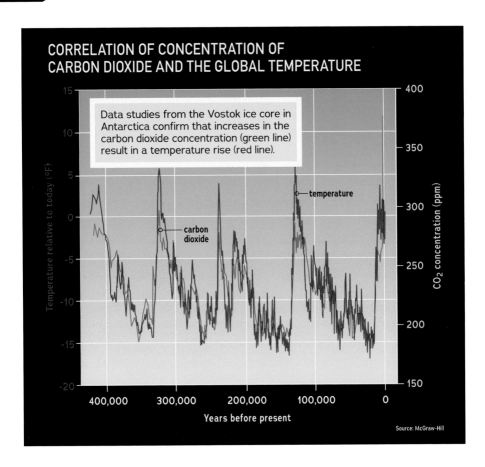

CORRELATION OF CONCENTRATION OF CARBON DIOXIDE AND THE GLOBAL TEMPERATURE

Data studies from the Vostok ice core in Antarctica confirm that increases in the carbon dioxide concentration (green line) result in a temperature rise (red line).

temperature

carbon dioxide

Temperature relative to today (°F)

CO_2 concentration (ppm)

Years before present

Source: McGraw-Hill

Methane comes from different sources. If organic matter decays in the absence of oxygen, it produces methane. For example, methane (sometimes called marsh gas) is produced when plant matter decays in the stagnant (deprived of oxygen) waters of a wetland or marsh. One-quarter of all methane emissions in the atmosphere naturally bubbles up from wetlands. The other major sources of methane are anthropogenic (created by humans). They are associated with farming (cows and rice paddies). Crude oil and natural gas contain methane, which is gaseous and easily escapes into the atmosphere. Methane is released when fossil fuels are taken out of the ground until they are finally used. It is released during mining, refining, transport, fracking, and energy production.

Livestock animals are a major nonhuman source of methane emissions, contributing about one-third of total methane emissions. Many animals, particularly cattle and sheep, have a rumen (the first part of their stomach). There, bacteria and other microorganisms break down cellulose from the grasses and leaves the animals eat. A by-product of this digestion is methane. The animals release it through belching and flatulence. An average cow emits 66 gallons (250 L) of methane every day. Earth has about 1.5 billion cows. That's about 100 billion gallons (375 billion L) of methane every day!

Rice paddies, where farmers grow rice, are much like wetlands. Rice requires a lot of water to grow, but most of the water in the paddies is stagnant. With little oxygen in the standing water, other small plants or weeds in the paddies decay and release methane.

Methane forms in stagnant bodies of water such as in these rice paddies in Thailand.

The only sink for atmospheric methane is the hydroxyl radical (OH·). It is formed by ultraviolet light reacting with oxygen and water. The reaction lasts less than a second, and its concentration has been fairly constant. So, while methane emissions are increasing, the sink is remaining constant. This results in a net increase in methane.

EARTH'S RISING TEMPERATURES

The National Aeronautics and Space Administration (NASA) does a monthly analysis of global temperatures. Researchers assemble the data from various sources. They include sixty-three hundred meteorological stations around the world, ship- and buoy-based instruments measuring sea surface temperatures, and Antarctic research stations. In the 136 years of NASA temperature records, 16 of the 17 warmest years have occurred since 2001. (The one exception was 1998.) The year 2016 had the hottest global average temperature—1.7°F (0.9°C) higher than the 1880 to 2017 average temperature—in recorded history. The high temperature was largely due to increases in carbon dioxide and methane levels. A strong El Niño—a warming phase of a Pacific Ocean climate cycle—added to the heat that year.

The average global temperature on Earth has increased by about 1.5°F (0.85°C) since 1880. That year the International Meteorological Organization began standardizing the recording of global temperatures. Two-thirds of that warming has occurred since 1975, at a rate of roughly 0.3°F to 0.4°F (0.15°C to 0.20°C) per decade.

The North Pole and South Pole have experienced the largest temperature increases. The warming has led to significant melting of sea ice. Perennial, or year-round, sea ice in the Arctic is declining at a rate of 9 percent per decade. Long-term temperature forecasts predict a rise of 2.5°F to 10°F (1.4°C to 5.6°C) over the next century. This may seem like a small temperature change, but a one- to two-degree drop was all it took to move Earth into the Little Ice Age seven hundred years ago. As predicted in earlier studies, these small changes can have significant local impact. As temperatures warm, glaciers are shrinking, ice on rivers and lakes is breaking up earlier every year, plant and animal ranges have shifted, and trees are flowering sooner each year. The melting of sea ice results in an accelerated global rise in sea levels. Heat waves are longer and more intense. And scientists have shown that climate change is associated with an increase in extreme weather events. Most, but not all, are due to temperature increases. For example, the National Oceanic and Atmospheric Administration has recorded the number and the cost of all weather-related disasters that have occurred in the United States since 1980. From 1980 to 2017, the agency recorded 212 weather disasters that have cost more than $1 billion each. The total cost of the events exceeded $1.2 trillion. The 1980 to 2016 annual average was 5.5 events per year. It increased to 10.6 events for 2012 to 2016.

With climate change, the number and intensity of storms is increasing. Snowstorms, for example, are dumping unheard of amounts of snow, sometimes in regions that usually have little if any snow every year.

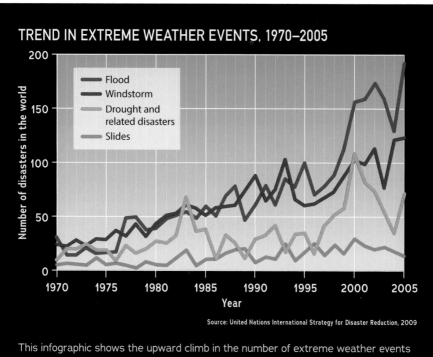

TREND IN EXTREME WEATHER EVENTS, 1970–2005

Number of disasters in the world

- Flood
- Windstorm
- Drought and related disasters
- Slides

Year

Source: United Nations International Strategy for Disaster Reduction, 2009

This infographic shows the upward climb in the number of extreme weather events over the course of thirty-five years. Scientists attribute the rise to climate change.

FINDING SOLUTIONS

Lawmakers pass laws and make regulations to help control the release of toxic and other harmful chemicals into the atmosphere and into the planet's waters. The EPA, with regional and state offices, is the main environmental regulation agency in the United States. Among other things, it oversees the two main US environmental laws—the Clean Air Act (1955) and the Clean Water Act (1948). The two laws, which have been amended, set rules for air quality, covering auto and airplane emissions and noise pollution. Some of the rules for water quality include acceptable concentrations of heavy metals, wastewater standards for municipal and industrial waste, and the preservation of wetlands.

The laws have been very successful, and the concentrations of pollutants regulated by the acts have dropped over time. To slow down climate change, the EPA added carbon dioxide to the list of regulated gases in January 2011. In June 2014, the EPA also passed the Clean Power Plan to limit greenhouse gas emissions. However, in fall 2017, EPA chief Scott Pruitt—a Republican appointed by President Trump—repealed the plan. The repeal is at odds with the goals of the Clean Air Act and slows the move away from coal-powered plants. However, Pruitt and others who share his views feel the move will save money and help develop US energy resources.

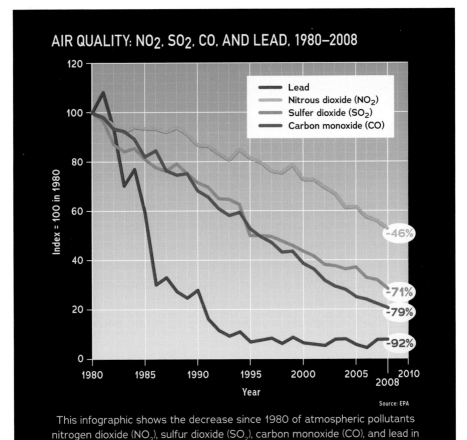

AIR QUALITY: NO_2, SO_2, CO, AND LEAD, 1980–2008

Lead
Nitrous dioxide (NO_2)
Sulfer dioxide (SO_2)
Carbon monoxide (CO)

Index = 100 in 1980

-46%
-71%
-79%
-92%

Year

This infographic shows the decrease since 1980 of atmospheric pollutants nitrogen dioxide (NO_2), sulfur dioxide (SO_2), carbon monoxide (CO), and lead in the United States due to stricter air quality regulations. As the amount of toxic pollutants in the air lowers, air quality improves.

Finding less polluting and renewable energy sources for homes, factories, and vehicles is key to addressing pollution and climate change. The amount of fossil fuels on Earth is naturally finite, or limited. So researchers are developing new sources of fuel that come from materials we can grow, make, or harness naturally without limit. These include wind, water, and solar power. They also include vegetable oils and animal grease! In 2017, 17 percent of all electricity in the United States was from renewable energy sources. However, they still only make up 4 percent of the global energy mix. The most remarkable shift away from coal and toward renewable energy and cleaner natural gas has been in the United Kingdom. It closed its last three underground coal mines in 2016. In 2012, 40 percent of all electricity in the United Kingdom came from coal-powered plants. By 2017 that number had dropped to 7 percent.

Renewable energy sources, especially solar radiation, have many advantages over fossil fuels. They are free and incredibly abundant. They have low environmental impact. They are far less expensive to produce. But they aren't always available consistently. For example, cloud cover reduces solar radiation, and if winds drop, the blades of wind turbines don't move. So efficient energy storage and backup systems are needed to provide a steady supply of energy. As innovators create solutions to these disadvantages, renewable energy is becoming a bigger part of the global energy mix.

HYBRID CARS

Cars account for 27 percent of the greenhouse emissions in the United States. Finding new ways to fuel cars is critical to reducing CO_2 emissions and addressing climate change. One innovation is the hybrid car. It relies on two or more sources of power for fuel. Most hybrid cars on the road are gasoline-electric hybrids. They use about 70 percent less gasoline than conventional models do. So these hybrids produce 70 percent less carbon dioxide.

Hybrid cars produce electrical energy from a battery and regenerative braking. When braking, a driver slows the car and removes kinetic energy from the car. (Kinetic energy comes from motion.) Most of that energy is lost as heat. This type of hybrid car captures the breaking energy and regenerates it, or redirects it to charge the battery. Hybrid cars are most efficient and use less fuel in city driving, which involves more braking than on the highway. This is the exact opposite of a conventional car, which uses more fuel in city driving, where most people do the bulk of their driving.

ELECTRIC CARS

Another alternative to gasoline-powered cars is electric cars. Electric motors with electric energy stored in rechargeable batteries propel these cars. The batteries power the car for a certain number of miles. Then the driver must plug the battery into a power outlet to recharge it. Plug-in hybrids use gasoline when they have no charge left in their battery. Electric cars give off zero tail pipe pollution, contributing no greenhouse gases or particulate matter to the atmosphere. And they are very quiet. But depending on the source of electricity for recharging the battery, these cars can be indirectly very polluting. For example, some drivers may live in an area where coal is the main source of power for electricity. Then coal, which is highly polluting, is powering that electric car. But if the source of electricity is green (wind, water, or solar), then electric cars are a very clean option.

In 2017 only 1.1 percent of all cars sold in the United States were electric or plug-in hybrids. This is because the batteries in electric cars are very expensive and recharging stations are not as common as gas stations. Recharging takes time too. Most car batteries are lithium (Li) batteries. They can be charged to 80 percent of their capacity in thirty minutes. Electric and hybrid cars also don't go as far as a gasoline-powered car. Generally, a gasoline tank holds enough fuel for between 250 to 375 miles (402 to 604 km). Electric and hybrid cars can only go about 150 to 200 miles (241 to 322 km) before requiring a recharge. But battery prices are dropping. They will continue to become cheaper and more efficient. Experts estimate that Earth has enough lithium to power four billion electric car batteries. China leads the world in sales of electric cars and buses.

BIOETHANOL

Another important alternative to fossil fuels lies in other sources of natural fuels. Fossil fuels get their energy from photosynthetic organisms that have been compressed underground for millions of years. Biofuels get their energy from photosynthetic plants, such as corn, grown to supply energy. However, to supply all the world's energy requirements, more than 10 percent of Earth's land surface would have to be used for biofuel production. About 11 percent of Earth's surface is being used for agriculture, and another 10 percent is not available. So biofuels are only part of the solution.

One major biofuel is ethanol (C_2H_5OH)—a colorless liquid that comes from corn and sugarcane. People have used bioethanol as an automotive fuel since the late nineteenth century. It is also the active ingredient of alcoholic beverages such as beer and wine. In North America, most bioethanol comes from the starch in kernels of corn. Getting pure ethanol from corn is very energy intensive. In North America, coal and natural gas are the main sources of energy required for the distillation of corn bioethanol. So ethanol production from corn is not always a green process. Growing corn requires huge amounts of water for irrigation. In tropical countries, bioethanol comes from fermentation of the juice of sugarcane. The process of obtaining bioethanol from sugarcane requires less energy and is much cleaner.

BIODIESEL

Corn and sugarcane contain ethanol. Other plants (such as soybeans) and many seeds (such as canola) contain natural oils that can be extracted and used as biofuels in diesel engines. The first diesel engines powered by peanut oil were introduced at the 1900 World Fair in Paris, France. The production of biodiesel is about three times as energy efficient as bioethanol. Soybeans and canola also require less fertilizer and less space to grow than corn does, so they are a greener option.

Modern diesel vehicles can't run on straight vegetable oils because those oils gel up in cold weather and block fuel filters. So producers make biodiesel blends by mixing biodiesel with diesel fuel. Diesel cars and trucks can run with 5 percent and 20 percent biodiesel blends. In the United States, soybeans (containing 20 percent oil) are the most common source of biodiesel. In Europe canola (40 percent oil) is the most common source. Animal fats and recycled restaurant grease also can be converted into biodiesel. Some boats and other vehicles can use those fuels. The US Navy is the world's largest user of biodiesel. It uses a blend of diesel (about 95 percent) and biodiesel (5 percent) to power its ships.

HYDROELECTRIC POWER

Cars and power plants produce the same amount of greenhouse gases, about 33 percent of the total each. Power stations produce the energy for electricity in homes and in industrial settings. The electricity powers many things, including lights, cooking stoves, and heating systems.

About 16 percent of all global electricity is hydroelectric, or produced through capturing the power of water. To harness this energy, hydroelectric plants direct downward-flowing water from waterfalls and dams through turbines. The water turns the blades of the turbines, which then drive an electric generator. This motor

ENERGY CONSUMPTION

The amount of energy used per person in different countries depends on the standard of living, the temperature, and the size of that country. The higher a nation's standard of living, the more appliances, devices, gadgets, cars, and other fuel-dependent items its population has. So the per capita (per person) energy use is higher than in nations where people have fewer items. Colder countries use more fuel for heating. The bigger the area of the nation, the more energy it consumes transporting goods across long distances.

Per capita energy use in the United States is about 301 million British thermal units (Btus). This usage is a little more than four times the world average of 74 million Btus per person and almost twice that in Germany, Britain, and Japan. The United States and China have about the same total amount of energy consumption. But the population of China is more than four times as large, so China's per capita energy use is less than one-quarter of that in the United States. US consumption, as shown below, is fueled mostly by petroleum and natural gas.

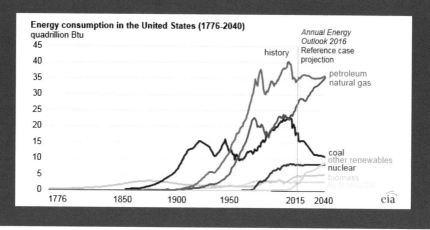

produces electricity. The amount of electric energy a plant can generate is proportional to the volume of water and the height from which it falls. So the more water and the greater the height from which it falls, the more electricity the plant can produce. Some of the world's biggest hydroelectric producers are in China and Brazil.

Hydroelectric dams are very flexible electricity sources. Within minutes they can go from producing no electricity to producing a full load. During low electricity demand, the excess power generated by dams can pump water into high-lying reservoirs (storage pools). When the energy demand increases again, that water can be released. It will flow through a turbine back down to the dam, producing more electricity during peak demand hours.

THREE GORGES DAM

Hydroelectric dams are not a completely clean source of energy. Nor are they without negative impact on communities, especially if poorly planned. To build them, construction companies usually flood large areas to create reservoirs of water. The reservoirs may

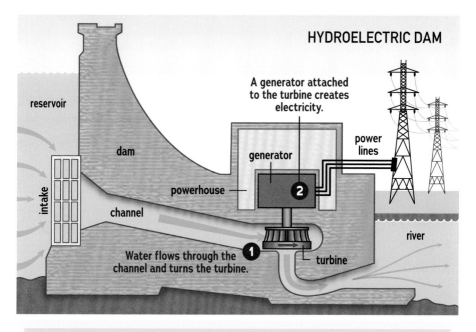

HYDROELECTRIC DAM

reservoir

A generator attached to the turbine creates electricity.

dam

generator

power lines

intake

powerhouse

channel

river

Water flows through the **1** channel and turns the turbine.

turbine

This infographic shows the basic workings of a hydroelectric dam. Water flows through the channel of the dam to turn a turbine, which then powers a generator to create electricity.

cover areas of natural beauty, endangered animal species, and even people's homes. Three Gorges Dam on the Yangtze River in Hubei Province, China, for example, was completed in 2006 after twelve years of construction. Some though not all critics have concerns about the environmental impact of the dam because of its massive scale. They fear the dam may be negatively impacting the region's ecology, geology, and climate. The dam project produces the most hydroelectric power of any plant in the world, with a reservoir lake that is more than 400 miles (644 km) long. But to make way for the lake, 1.2 million people—from thirteen cities, fourteen towns, and 1,350 villages—had to move. The water in the reservoir is often stagnant, causing low oxygen levels that kill plant and animal

Water rushes out of penstocks (channels) at Three Gorges Dam in China. Three Gorges is the world's largest power station, providing energy with thirty-two individual generators. In cases of extreme flooding from rainstorms, such as in 2017, the dam shuts down most of its generators to protect the dam's turbines.

life. The decaying plant matter releases large amounts of the greenhouse gas methane. The dams that form the lake also block the migratory routes of fishes. The weight of the dams, of tunnels for water, and of the reservoir has caused enormous geologic pressure that has led to massive landslides. Some of the landslides have killed people and weakened the dams. Yet many experts feel that Three Gorges is better for the environment overall than the alternative—coal.

WIND ENERGY

Three Gorges Dam has not been the renewable energy solution that some people thought it would be. But China is a global leader in renewable wind power. In 2015, for example, workers were installing two new wind turbines every hour in China. China produced 187.7 million megawatt hours (MWh) in 2017. The United States is a leader too. In 2016 it produced the second most power of any nation from wind, at more than 89 MWh. (Megawatt hours are a measure of the amount of electricity used over a period of time.)

Some wind farms are in offshore areas, where winds are strong and constant. But the construction and upkeep of turbines in the ocean is expensive. Ideal locations for wind farms are in areas that have constant, nonturbulent winds in all seasons. The Americas, western Europe, Russia, and China have winds that can be successfully harnessed. Africa, eastern Europe, and Southeast Asia have low wind-power potential. Generally, wind farms cover large areas because the wind turbines have to be at least seven rotor blade lengths apart. Wind farms work well with hydroelectric power plants. When winds drop, water can be released in a dam to create backup electricity. The two sources together create an even, predictable power supply.

Wind power is one of the most economical forms of renewable energy, and CO_2 emissions from wind power are the lowest for any power source. Globally, wind farms produce 2.5 percent of electrical power. Experts say that someday wind power could supply about one-fifth of the world's electricity needs. In the United States, wind power creates close to 5 percent of all the electricity produced in the nation. Some states are leading the way. For example, more than 31 percent of the electricity generated in Iowa comes from wind. And Kansas and South Dakota generate more than 20 percent of their electricity from wind.

Like hydroelectricity, wind-powered electricity is generated by turbines. In wind farms, large turbines stand tall. The tallest wind turbines in the United States are twenty stories high and have blades the length of football fields. Wind turns the large blades of the turbines. They spin, turning a shaft attached to a nearby generator that makes electricity. They can generate enough electricity for fourteen hundred US homes. The Gansu Wind Farm Project in desert areas near Jiuquan, China, has seven thousand wind turbines and is the largest wind farm in the world. Yet demand for wind power in China is not as great as leaders had hoped. Many manufacturers still rely on coal, even though it contributes to China's high levels of greenhouse gas emissions. (China emits the highest level of greenhouse gases of any nation on Earth.) The nation does not have enough power lines to carry the wind-power electricity to its fast-growing cities. So although China is taking the lead in creating renewable energy, the country is not yet able to make significant reductions in air pollution and carbon emissions.

SOLAR ENERGY

Innovators are also looking to solar energy for green solutions. More energy from the sun reaches Earth in one hour than all humans on the planet use from fossil fuels in one year. And photosynthesis uses up only 0.35 percent of the sun's energy. That leaves a lot of energy that can be harnessed.

Some states combine wind and solar farms. When one source of energy is temporarily stalled by lack of wind or by a cloudy day, the other source functions as a backup to avoid interruptions of service. These photovoltaic solar panels and wind turbines are at the San Gorgonio Pass Wind Farm near Palm Springs, California. The solar installation has a 2.3 MW capacity.

The sun's energy is mostly visible radiation with a little ultraviolet light and infrared radiation. Solar radiation can be used in various ways. Thermal solar power is a technology for absorbing the sun's radiation in a solar panel so it can create heat to warm water for household use or to produce electrical energy. Photoconversion is a technology in which a photovoltaic cell absorbs visible and UV radiation to excite electrons to create electricity.

At its simplest, solar radiation can be used directly. For example, workers can install a series of flat black solar panels, facing the sun, onto a roof of a building to absorb sunlight. Pumps, typically in the attic of the building, direct water over the hot

GREEN CITIES OF THE WORLD

Canada

NORTH AMERICA

Iceland

United States

Almost half of Brazil's greenest cities are powered entirely by hydropower.

Mexico

Venezuela

Panama

This map highlights cities of the world that generate a substantial amount of electricity (70 to 100 percent) from renewable sources of energy.

Colombia

Equador

SOUTH AMERICA

Brazil

Chile

Paraguay

Source: Carbon Disclosure Project (CDP) Worldwide

black solar panels. The water heats up naturally and flows back through pipes for immediate use. Or the hot water can be kept in a storage tank until needed. The temperature of the roof-mounted solar panels is never more than the boiling point of water (212°F, or 100°C).

Sweden
Norway
Denmark
Switzerland
Slovenia
EUROPE Romania
Portugal
Sardinia
Italy
ASIA
South Korea
AFRICA
Ethiopia
Kenya
Cameroon
Tanzania
Mozambique
Zimbabwe
AUSTRALIA
New Zealand
Tasmania

Percentage of electricity in the greenest cities that comes from renewables
○ 70 to 79 percent △ 80 to 89 percent ▢ 90 to 99 percent ★ 100 percent

Steam turbines that generate electricity need water to be at much higher temperatures. So they will rely on concentrated solar thermal systems. These setups collect and focus sunlight from a large array of hundreds of solar mirrors. The rotating mirrors follow the sun and reflect all the sunlight to heat some centrally located water pipes. Water heated by concentrated systems can reach very high temperatures—above 2,192°F (1,200°C). The steam from superhot water is perfect for driving steam turbines to generate electricity, and solar-generated steam is far cleaner than coal-generated steam.

Cool water is also required in concentrated solar plants. For efficiency, the power plants recycle water from the steam they create. The plants pump cold water into pipes that cool the steam after it has turned a turbine. The steam condenses back into water. Concentrated sunlight then reheats it to create more steam to keep the turbine turning. However, deserts and other locations that have a lot of direct sunlight and space for concentrated solar plants often don't have enough rivers and lakes to provide cooling water. So concentrated solar plants aren't very common.

PHOTOVOLTAIC TECHNOLOGY

Most photovoltaic cells, used for photoconversion, have two layers of doped silicon (Si) crystals. In doping, chemical impurities are added to the silicon. A silicon atom has fourteen electrons. The top layer of silicon is doped with an element, such as phosphorous, that has one more electron than silicon does. The bottom layer of silicon is doped with an element such as boron that has one less available electron. The layer doped with phosphorous will be slightly more negatively (n) charged than pure silicon. So scientists call it the n-layer. The bottom layer has fewer electrons and is slightly more positively (p) charged. So scientists call it the p-layer. Between the two layers is the P-N junction. This junction is the area where the p and n layers meet. The P-N junction only allows electrons to flow from the p-layer to the n-layer but not from the n-layer to the p-layer.

When sunlight hits a photovoltaic cell, electrons are released. Electrons are negatively charged, so the electrons in the n-layer are attracted to the positive p-layer. But the n-layer electrons can't cross the P-N junction. So an external circuit (a thin wire) from the n-layer to the p-layer allows the electrons to travel from the n- to the p-layer through the wire. As long as the sun shines on the cell, electrons are released and travel through the wire. This movement of electrons creates a small electrical current. Individual photovoltaic cells are just a few inches large and don't generate much electricity. But many photovoltaic cells combined together in a solar panel combined into larger solar arrays can create large amounts of electricity. The world's largest solar park—known informally as the Great Wall of Solar—is in Zhongwei, China. It can generate 1,547 megawatts.

Solar panels do not generate any greenhouse gases. But manufacturing the panels requires significant energy. Solar energy is more CO_2-intensive than wind energy. And silicon photovoltaic cells have low efficiencies of 15 to 20 percent. They lose more than 80 percent of the sun's energy. Researchers are looking for cheaper and more efficient materials to replace silicon crystals in photoconversion solar panels.

Using current technologies, a continuous array of photovoltaic solar cells covering an area of 100 x 100 miles (26,000 sq. km) would generate all the energy needs of the United States. But it would cost trillions of dollars to construct, so the United States would probably never go 100 percent solar. Solar is growing, and in 2015, half a million solar panels were installed every day.

WHAT CAN YOU DO?

For the first time ever, in 2017, wind and sun together met more than 10 percent of US electricity needs. Iowa is a leader among the fifty states, getting 37 percent of its electricity from a combination of wind and solar sources. Here are some things you can do in your own life to make a difference and leave a smaller carbon footprint.

To live a greener life, try out these ideas:

- To use less fuel, walk, bike, carpool, or take public transportation whenever you can.
- To use less electricity, turn off lights and electronic devices when you aren't using them. Don't just put your device in sleep mode either. Turn it off completely, and unplug your chargers when you aren't using them.
- Eliminate as much plastic from your life as you can. Plastic is petroleum based. Use reusable metal or glass containers for coffee and other beverages. Use glass containers for leftovers and lunches. Use paper sandwich bags instead of plastic. Say no to plastic straws and bags!
- Start a Boomerang Bag club in your neighborhood. Founded in Australia, this global grassroots group is devoted to removing plastic from the consumer cycle. Community groups get together to make cloth tote bags (*right*) from recycled and donated fabrics. Check out boomerangbags.org to learn more.

- Don't drink bottled water. Unless the bottle says "spring water," or "artesian water," it comes from tap water anyway. Fossil fuels have been used to deliver the bottles—most of which are plastic—across the country to a store near you. Plastics are petroleum products from fossil fuels. Every minute, more than one million plastic bottles are sold. More than 90 percent of the bottles aren't recycled, and it takes them four hundred years to decompose. In 2050 the ocean probably will have more plastic by mass than fish.

- Bring your own cloth bag when you shop. Don't use plastic or paper bags.
- Practice the three Rs—reduce, reuse, and recycle. Whatever you can do to slow down consumption reduces waste and your carbon footprint.
- Speak up. Talk to friends, family, neighbors, and people at school about going green. Work together to make changes in your school and neighborhood.
- Help local politicians who support green practices. When you are old enough, vote for them.

French physicist Henri Becquerel made one of the world's greatest scientific discoveries—by accident. In 1896, when he was a new professor of physics at the École Polytechnique in Paris, Becquerel discovered that the heavy metal uranium (U) releases a form of radiation that he could capture on a photographic plate. He bought his plates from the Lumière brothers, Auguste and Louis, famous in cinema history as the world's first filmmakers.

Photographic plates had to be protected from light. So Becquerel wrapped his plates in paper and stored them in a desk drawer. He was a meticulous man and was surprised when he went to use his plates that they seemed to have been exposed to light.

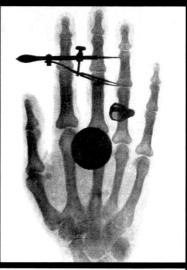

Physicist Henri Becquerel (*left*) accidentally discovered radioactivity in the late nineteenth century. At just about the same time, German physicist Wilhelm Röntgen became the first person to detect X-rays. He used the technology to scan his wife's hand (*right*) in 1896, the same year Becquerel discovered radioactivity. Both men were awarded Nobel Prizes for their discoveries.

When he noticed it a second time, Becquerel was intrigued. He believed that the plates couldn't have been exposed to light. So he started to experiment. He discovered that when he placed his photographic plates in the drawer close to pitchblende (a uranium-rich mineral), the plates were exposed. It was as if the rocks were emitting an invisible light. Becquerel realized that what he had discovered was not X-ray radiation. It was something new, something that physicist Marie Curie would later name radioactivity.

Marie Curie and her husband, Pierre, were physics professors at the Sorbonne University in Paris. They focused their research on the newly discovered phenomenon. They worked in laboratories with no protection against exposure to radiation. (The dangers of radiation weren't yet known.) The two scientists discovered two new elements—polonium (Po) and radium (Ra)—that are both radioactive. Marie Curie developed methods for separating radium (Ra) from all the other elements in radium-containing minerals. She carefully studied radium and its radioactivity. For her studies of radioactivity, Curie received two Nobel Prizes—one in physics (in 1903, which she shared with her husband and with Becquerel) and the other in chemistry (in 1911). She died in 1934 from a type of anemia resulting from long-term exposure to radiation.

Marie Curie is pictured in this image from about 1903 with her husband, Pierre, in the laboratory. Marie Curie and her husband won the 1903 Nobel Prize in Physics. After his death in 1906, she won the 1911 Nobel Prize in Chemistry.

MADAME CURIE

Maria Sklodowska was born on November 7, 1867, in Warsaw, Poland. Because women were barred from studying at the University of Warsaw, she moved to Paris with her sister Bronya. Maria worked as a governess to support her sister's medical school studies. In 1891 her sister graduated, Maria changed her name to Marie (the French version of Maria), and she started her studies at the Sorbonne. Marie studied radioactivity and met her future husband, Pierre Curie, through a mutual friend. In 1903 she earned her PhD from the University of Paris with a dissertation titled "Research on Radioactive Substances." That year she was also jointly awarded the Nobel Prize in Physics with her husband and Henri Becquerel for their studies on radiation. Getting a Nobel Prize and a PhD in the same year had never happened before or since.

Based on her achievements, Curie became the chair of the Sorbonne Physics Department in 1906. That year a horse-drawn carriage hit her husband, who died instantly. Five years later, in 1911, Marie Curie was awarded a second Nobel Prize, this time in chemistry, "in recognition of her services to the advancement of chemistry by the discovery of the elements radium and polonium, by the isolation of radium and the study of the nature and compounds of this remarkable element."

Curie was the first woman awarded a Nobel Prize in Chemistry. Since 1911 the committee has awarded the Nobel Prize in Chemistry to only three other women. One was the Curies' eldest daughter, Irène Joliot-Curie, in 1935. She also worked with radioactive isotopes. Both Marie Curie and Irène Joliot-Curie died from a type of anemia caused by radioactive isotopes. Marie Curie's notebooks are still so radioactive they have to be stored in lead-lined boxes. Without protection, it is dangerous to read them and will remain dangerous for the next thousand years.

Working separately from each other and at the same time as the Curies, New Zealand-born physicist Ernest Rutherford and French physicist Paul Villard discovered three types of radiation. Rutherford named them alpha, beta, and gamma particles after the first three letters of the Greek alphabet. All occur naturally as part of radioactive decay. Alpha particles have two protons and two neutrons held together in a way that resembles the nucleus of the isotope helium-4. (Isotopes are different forms of the same element that have the same numbers of protons but different numbers of neutrons in their nuclei.) Alpha particles have no electrons. A beta particle is a high-speed electron. It is released when a neutron in a radioactive nucleus such as potassium-40 spontaneously splits into a proton and an electron. Gamma radiation is electromagnetic radiation in the form of photon rays. With very short wavelengths, gamma rays are the most high-energy form of electromagnetic radiation. They have large amounts of energy and no mass.

NUCLEAR CHEMISTRY

Nuclear chemistry is the study of changes that occur in the nucleus of an atom. Protons in a nucleus are positively charged, and they naturally repel one another. That is where neutrons come in. They get in between the positively charged protons and weaken the natural repulsion among protons. They can also interchange with protons. The bigger an atom (the larger its atomic number), the more protons it has and therefore the more neutrons between the protons. Hydrogen is the smallest atom, with just one proton, and it has no neutrons in the nucleus. The isotope uranium-235 has 92 protons to its 143 neutrons. (You can do the math to see how the numbers fit together: 92 + 143 = 235.) In an atom with this many protons, the repulsion between the protons is overwhelming. So the nucleus becomes unstable and falls apart, forming smaller nuclei. Scientists call this process nuclear fission. It creates radioactive energy, and scientists can make it happen on purpose.

PUTTING RADIOACTIVE MATERIALS TO USE

More than forty million medical procedures a year use radioactive isotopes. They are used to diagnose and image (scan for) diseases and conditions of all kinds, from brain tumors to thyroid cancers. X-rays and other forms of radiation rely on external sources for their radiation.

WHAT ARE ISOTOPES?

The periodic table shows all the symbols of the known elements. It also includes each element's atomic number (Z, or the number of protons) and its mass number (A, the number of protons and neutrons). The table does not list the number of neutrons in an element. The difference between the mass number and the atomic number (A minus Z) is the number of neutrons. Some elements have different numbers of neutrons. Scientists call them isotopes. For example, hydrogen (atomic number 1) occurs naturally in three different isotopes, with mass numbers 1, 2, and 3. Scientists write them as hydrogen-1, hydrogen-2, and hydrogen-3. Each number refers to the mass number (A). All forms of hydrogen have one electron and one proton (atomic number Z = 1) but differ in the number of neutrons. Hydrogen-1 is the most common form, with just one proton (and one electron). It has no neutrons (A minus Z, or 1 minus 1, = 0). Hydrogen-2, with one proton, has one neutron (A minus Z, or 2 minus 1, = 1). Hydrogen-3, also with one proton, has two neutrons (A minus Z, or 3 minus 1, = 2).

Uranium-235 is a rare isotope. Only 0.7 percent of naturally occurring uranium is made up of the U-235 isotope. The most naturally occurring uranium is the U-238 isotope. It does not undergo nuclear fission. To have a self-sustaining fission reaction, as required in a nuclear power plant, at least 3 to 5 percent of the uranium has to be U-235. Less than that is not

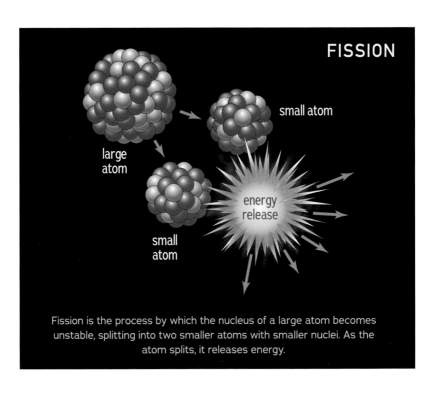

FISSION

small atom

large
atom

energy
release

small
atom

Fission is the process by which the nucleus of a large atom becomes
unstable, splitting into two smaller atoms with smaller nuclei. As the
atom splits, it releases energy.

enough for the neutrons released in a fission reaction to start a new reaction. Without a chain reaction, the nuclear fission is not self-sustaining.

ENRICHMENT

A nuclear bomb works differently from a nuclear power plant. At the power station, plant operators carefully control the reactions. But in a nuclear bomb, every neutron has to start a new reaction to generate a huge amount of energy very quickly—without any control. Nuclear weapons require highly enriched uranium made from 25 to 90 percent U-235. Enriching uranium is very technically demanding. It involves separating U-235 from U-238 isotopes of uranium. Common techniques include centrifugation (spinning a gaseous sample of UF_6 around so fast that the heavier UF_6 with U-238 separates from the lighter UF_6 with U-235). Another technique is gaseous diffusion, or the net movement of molecules from a region of high concentration (through a membrane) to a region of low concentration due to random motion of the molecules through thousands of membranes.

Fewer than twenty countries in the world are able to enrich uranium. Some of these countries sell enriched uranium to other nations for their nuclear power plants. They don't sell highly enriched uranium that can be used to make nuclear weapons. North Korea is the most recent nation to build a nuclear enrichment facility. Since 2018 North Korea has a functioning nuclear power plant and a nuclear bomb.

Radioactive isotopes can be injected into the body to release the radioactive particles (mainly gamma particles) from the inside. About 80 percent of all radioisotopic procedures use technecium-99m. It's used in many procedures such as to image blood flowing through the brain or the heart.

One of the most significant uses of nuclear fission was the development of the nuclear bomb toward the end of World War II. The global war—fought across Europe and Asia—had taken millions of lives by early 1945. Leaders thought they would lose millions more. Scientists knew they could create and control nuclear fission to create devastating atomic weapons. On July 16, 1945, the first nuclear bomb exploded as a test in the New Mexico desert. The American Manhattan Project had achieved its goal. US president Harry S. Truman decided to drop two atomic bombs on Japan in

August 1945, one on Hiroshima (August 6, 1945) and the other on Nagasaki (August 9, 1945). About two hundred thousand people died. Japan announced its surrender days later, on August 15, and the war ended.

Fission technology for nuclear weapons relies on U-235. After the war, scientists developed another nuclear technology—fusion. Fission reactions come from large nuclei, such as U-235, falling apart because they are unstable. Fusion reactions get their energy from merging two small nuclei (with low atomic numbers). On November 1, 1952, the United States tested the world's first full-scale thermonuclear fusion, or hydrogen bomb. It was four hundred times more powerful than the nuclear bomb dropped on Nagasaki. By the year 2017, various nations had developed just over 9,220 nuclear weapons. About 95 percent of them are in the United States and Russia. France, China, the United Kingdom, Pakistan, India, Israel, and North Korea also have them.

NUCLEAR ENERGY

Nuclear power also is used for peaceful purposes around the world. Through controlled nuclear fission at nuclear power plants, uranium-235 can generate two to three million times more energy than an equivalent amount of oil or coal. Nuclear power plants release only a minimal amount of greenhouse gases. So generating electricity the nuclear way is a very attractive option for many communities. But nuclear power plants produce waste products that give off harmful radiation for thousands of years. And nuclear disasters can cause significantly more harm if something goes wrong than anything associated with other energy sources.

In a controlled way at nuclear power plants, devices called startup neutron sources shoot neutrons into uranium-235 nuclei. When a neutron hits a U-235 nucleus, an unstable uranium-236 nucleus forms. It quickly falls apart to form two new nuclei and two

Cooling towers in Belleville-sur-Loire, France, rise in a field. France generates about 75 percent of its electricity from nuclear power. The nation's long-term goal, however, is to reduce dependence on nuclear energy to allow for the growth of greener energy sources.

or three new neutrons. When the newly created neutrons hit another uranium-235 nucleus, a new reaction begins and creates more nuclei and releases more neutrons. These neutrons can in turn start their own reactions, resulting in a chain reaction in which every reaction starts a new reaction—each one releasing energy as heat. A chain reaction is a bit like a chain of dominoes, where knocking over the first domino leads to the entire chain of dominoes falling over. But in a nuclear power plant, the system is controlled so that each reaction starts just one new reaction. If it created more than that, millions of reactions would occur within a second, creating uncontrollable energy, such as that released in a nuclear bomb.

Once the nuclear reaction starts, it continues until the supply of U-235 nuclei runs out. In a nuclear power plant, engineers make sure that the nuclear reactions are self-sustaining. They watch to make sure that only some of the released neutrons start their own

HALF-LIVES

The half-life $(t_{1/2})$ of a radioactive element is the length of time it takes for the level of that element's radioactivity to drop by one-half. Half-lives range from less than one second to billions of years. In two half-lives, the radioactivity will have fallen to one-quarter of an element's original level. After seven half-lives, the radioactive element will be giving off less than 1 percent of its initial radiation.

Some doctors use radioisotopes in their work. These elements have half-lives that are just long enough to be in the body for the length of the procedure. For example, technecium-99m is used for imaging and has a half-life of just six hours.

Iodine-131 $(t_{1/2} = 8$ days), cesium-134 $(t_{1/2} = 2$ years), cesium-137 $(t_{1/2} = 30$ years), and strontium-90 $(t_{1/2} = 29$ years) were the most dangerous isotopes released in the Chernobyl and Fukushima disasters. Their half-lives are long enough that they can spread far from the accident sites, where people breathe them in or they enter the food chain. From inside the human body, they give off harmful radiation. Spent fuel contains a wide variety of radioisotopes. Some have long half-lives and give off radiation for thousands of years. So long-term safe storage of nuclear waste is very important.

reactions. That way the plant can control the number of reactions and the amount of energy the reactions produce. Nuclear power plants pay careful attention to the number of reactions, because if they increase uncontrollably, a dangerous explosion will occur.

Nuclear power plants are all about controlling the number of neutrons available to start new reactions. The reactions release energy in the form of heat, which the plant uses to boil water to create steam. Like any other steam-based energy system, the pressure of the steam powers a turbine that in turn fuels a generator to create electricity.

The uranium fuel in a nuclear power plant comes in the form of small nuclear fuel pellets about the size of a coin. The pellets are stacked on top of one another in fuel rods. Each rod contains about two hundred pellets of enriched U-235, and each nuclear reactor can house thousands of fuel rods. Among the fuel rods in

the reactors are control rods. These rods are filled with neutron-absorbing boron or cadmium pellets. Raising or lowering the control rods controls the speed of the nuclear reactions by controlling the number of free neutrons. Ideally, neutrons are absorbed so that each reaction starts about one new reaction. Then the reaction does not expand to start more than one reaction. To increase the energy, plant operators use remote controls to lift up the control rods so that neutrons in the fuel rods can travel freely among the U-235 pellets. Many fission reactions occur, producing a lot of energy. In an emergency or when the fuel rods need to be changed, a plant operator can stop all the reactions. The operator lowers all the control rods back into place, which totally stops the flow of neutrons. The control rods will absorb the neutrons and quench the reactions.

Water pipes surround all the fuel and control rods. They prevent the reactor core from getting too hot. They absorb the heat from the nuclear fission reactions. They transfer that heat to water in a piece of equipment called a heat exchanger. The water in the reactor core is kept at very high pressures so it will stay in liquid

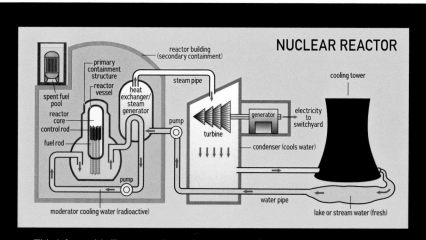

This infographic illustrates the main segments of a nuclear reactor. Fuel rods are contained in a water-filled core (*left*). Steam from the core turns a turbine (*center*), which then powers the generator (*right*) that creates electricity.

form in the high temperatures of the core. (Water under pressure boils at much higher temperatures than if it is not under pressure.) The water in the heat exchanger is at much lower pressure so the hot water from the core rapidly heats it to the boiling point. This creates the steam to power the turbine. The reactor core is highly radioactive. So the water that cools the core and the water in the heat exchanger are in closed circuits that are never released into the environment.

SPENT FUEL RODS

After several years in a nuclear reactor, the amount of U-235 in the fuel pellets is spent. It no longer produces enough new reactions to create energy. Then the plant removes the rods and replaces them with new ones.

Spent fuel rods are hot. Nuclear fission is no longer taking place, but the unstable nuclei produced by previous nuclear fission reactions continue to release radiation and heat. Before they cool down, spent fuel rods can reach temperatures of up to 2,732°F (1,500°C). To cool them, the power plant places the spent fuel rods in racks and immerses them in large pools of cold circulating water. The water cools the rods and absorbs the radiation. The racks contain boron, which absorbs the radioactive neutrons. Globally, nuclear power plants have so far produced more than 330,000 tons (299,371 t) of spent fuel rods.

In the United States, most spent fuel rods are stored on-site in cooling pools at nuclear power plants. After ten to twenty years, the rods can be removed from the cooling pools and placed in dry, well-protected storage containers, or casks. The casks are sometimes stored at the nuclear power plant itself or at other approved sites. The sites have to be monitored and protected from natural disasters such as fires, earthquakes, and floods.

After ten years, most of the radioactivity in the spent fuel rods comes from cesium-137 and strontium-90. These are both beta emitters. They are particularly dangerous because they can enter the human body. Strontium is chemically very similar to calcium. If a human body is exposed to strontium, the radioactive strontium will replace calcium in bones and teeth. Cesium is similar to potassium, found in most animal cells. If a human or animal is exposed to cesium-137, it will replace the potassium. Radiation from strontium-90 can lead to bone cancer and leukemia. Radiation from cesium-137 causes a variety of cancers.

RADIATION DANGERS

Doctors use radiation in a safe and controlled way to diagnose and treat a range of conditions and diseases. But uncontrolled, unexpected, and high levels of exposure to radiation—whether to alpha, beta, or gamma rays—can lead to cancer and other diseases. If ovaries or testes (female and male reproductive organs) are exposed to radiation, health defects will appear in future generations.

Alpha and beta particles are not necessarily harmful. But when emitted from a radioactive nucleus during fission or decay—or in an accident—they are expelled at great speed. The energy from this speed (kinetic energy) can cause great damage. If radiation hits cells in a human, animal, or plant, the harm can include severe burns, diseases, or death.

Alpha particles are relatively large and very damaging. But they don't penetrate far because air, dead skin, and even clothing can stop them. So they tend to cause only limited damage, such as skin cancers. However, if alpha particles get deep into a body—from inhaling radioactive isotopes such as radon that produce alpha particles—they can cause a lot of damage inside the body. Radon causes about twenty thousand lung cancer deaths a year in the United States.

Beta particles move faster and are smaller than alpha particles. So they are more penetrating and can pass through clothes. Thin sheets of metal can stop them. Like alpha particles, beta particles are most damaging when inhaled or ingested through contaminated food. Gamma rays are the smallest, fastest, and the most penetrating of all forms of radiation. They can pass through concrete and deep into the body. This makes them the most dangerous form of radiation.

It takes hundreds of thousands of years for the radiation of the spent fuel rods to fall back to the levels of the original uranium from which it was extracted. Scientists and government officials do not agree on the safest procedure for long-term storage of nuclear waste. In the United States, nuclear waste is building up at individual nuclear power plants. The plants weren't designed to handle high volumes of it. Long-term solutions could include underground storage. But that would mean transporting nuclear waste across country and finding a community that is prepared to have casks of depleted fuel rods buried in their "backyards." In 1987, for example, the US Congress determined that Yucca Mountain in Nevada would be the permanent home for all the nation's spent fuel casks. The government spent more than $15 billion studying the site and found it to be safe. To date, politicians and voters in Nevada have kept the nuclear waste out of their state. But the pressure is building for them to allow the burial of nuclear waste deep within Yucca Mountain.

CHERNOBYL

Nuclear power plants, if well maintained and supervised, can be an efficient and clean method of producing electricity. It does not rely on fossil fuels nor does it release any greenhouse gases. However, the risks and dangers of nuclear accidents are real. In fact, they have already happened, with devastating consequences.

On April 26, 1986, management at the V. I. Lenin Nuclear Power Station in Chernobyl, Ukraine, was scheduled to do an experiment. It would test whether backup generators for the pumps that circulated water through the nuclear core could be up to speed in forty-five seconds. The speed is important in case of a power outage in the regular generators. At Chernobyl the regular generators got up to speed immediately. But doing so quickly wore out the generators, and they had to be frequently replaced.

A similar experiment in 1984, when the plant's fuel rods were spent, failed because the fuel in the rods didn't have enough neutrons to drive nuclear fission. Many of the workers involved in the 1984 experiment were fired.

By spring 1986, the fuel rods at the plant were again spent and needed to be replaced. The workers who were going to oversee the April 26 experiment knew what had happened in 1984. They were concerned about keeping their jobs. To make sure that nuclear fission wasn't quenched during the experiment, they overrode a number of the plant's safety mechanisms. For example, they slowed the water flowing through the core and withdrew most of the control rods from the reactor core. The slowed water could not absorb all the heat from the increased reactions. At 1:23 p.m., the crew leader at the plant noticed the rising temperature of the water. He dropped all the control rods, hoping to stop the chain reactions. However, it was too late. The reactor overheated, the control rods buckled and bent, and the water boiled and became steam. In just one and a half seconds, the power output of the reactor rose to 120 times its normal output. The pressure created by the steam was so enormous that it blew the 1,000-ton (907 t) concrete reactor lid off the top of the reactor core. Hot pieces of the radioactive core spewed out of the nuclear reactor and started numerous fires. The force of the explosion was so great that some of the radioactive debris blew 0.75 miles (1,200 m) into the sky. The radioactive debris spread as far away as Greece to the south and to Finland and Sweden to the northwest.

After the explosion, helicopters flew over the reactor. They dropped sand, lead, and other neutron-absorbing substances onto the reactor to extinguish the fire and prevent more radiation from escaping. Coal miners dug underneath the reactor's core so that workers could pump liquid nitrogen into the core to cool the nuclear fuel. In all, the explosion released 30 tons (27 t) of highly contaminated dust. It also released 5 percent (11 tons, or 9.6 t) of the radioactive material contained in reactor 4.

Ukrainian leaders knew they had to close off the radioactive core to prevent the spread of more radioactive materials to neighboring areas. So the Ukranian government built a large concrete structure called a sarcophagus around the nuclear reactor. By 1996 the sarcophagus itself was becoming radioactive and too dangerous to ignore. Over the next ten years, workers began building another sarcophagus to enclose the first one. To minimize exposure to radiation, the workers built the vast structure 328 yards (300 m) away from the disaster site. Then they moved the entire sarcophagus into its final place on November 29, 2016. Estimates suggest that the new sarcophagus will contain the radiation of the remaining nuclear material for about one hundred years. Experts believe that the ongoing cleanup at Chernobyl will take at least that long.

Until then an area of about 1,000 square miles (2,590 sq. km) around the power plant is too contaminated for human habitation. Most of the inhabitants of the area—about 300,000 people—were evacuated from this exclusion zone. Pripyat, for example, was a city in the center of what became the exclusion zone. Its population of 49,360 people was evacuated the day after the Chernobyl disaster, and it has been deserted ever since. However, just weeks after the evacuation, about one hundred people moved back into the exclusion zone. This had always been their home, and they were willing to risk nuclear contamination. Animals had not been removed from the exclusion zone. Without human competition, their numbers appear to be increasing. To better understand how plant and animal life has thrived in the disaster zone, researchers with the University of Georgia are studying the animals in the exclusion zone. They are able to monitor the movements of wolves, boars, foxes, and raccoon dogs with remotely operated cameras. Deformities and albinism in the animals have increased.

Workers walk past the new sarcophagus at the Chernobyl nuclear plant on April 26, 2017, the thirty-first anniversary of the Chernobyl disaster.

What was the human toll of the disaster? Thirty-one plant and rescue workers died from acute radiation sickness and burns they received the night of the explosion. Doctors in Ukraine and Belarus began to notice a sharp increase in childhood thyroid cancer four years after the disaster. In the years 1993 to 1997, the incidence of childhood thyroid cancer was especially high in areas of the Gomel region in Belarus, to the north of Chernobyl. There, cases of this cancer were about one hundred times higher than the usual incidence of this disease in children. Thyroid cancers are caused by exposure to iodine-131, which was released into the air during the Chernobyl catastrophe. Experts are also seeing certain types of leukemia among rescue workers who helped during the Chernobyl disaster. They can trace it back to radiation from the Chernobyl explosion. The International Atomic Energy Agency, the United Nations, and the World Health Organization estimate that cancers linked to the Chernobyl tragedy will have caused about nine thousand deaths. Most of them will be among plant and rescue workers and among residents who lived within a 100-mile (161 km) radius of the nuclear reactor during the disaster.

FUKUSHIMA

On March 11, 2011, a major earthquake occurred 60 miles (100 km) off the northeastern coast of Japan. As a precaution, operators at the Fukushima Daiichi nuclear power plant there shut down all its operations. The plant dropped all the control rods and quenched the nuclear fission reactions. Water continued to pump through the core. Even after chain reactions stop, reactor cores are still extremely hot. Radioactive emissions from fission products decrease significantly over time. But it can take years for the spent fuel rods to cool down completely. So they are kept in cooling pools for many years. Within an hour, the earthquake generated

Workers at the Tokyo Electric Power Company's Fukushima Daiichi nuclear power plant are part of a lengthy process of decontaminating and rebuilding the facility. As a result of the nuclear disaster in 2011, tens of thousands of people still live as evacuees away from contaminated areas.

a giant tsunami wave that was 42 feet (13 m) high when it hit the Fukushima power plant. The seawall near the power plant was designed only to protect against waves up to 18.7 feet (5.7 m). The wave that hit Fukushima was more than twice as high. It washed away the plant's generators and pumps. It destroyed the instrumentation that controlled the nuclear reactors at the site. In three of the reactors, the tsunami ripped out water pipes, so cooling water leaked out of the core.

The temperature inside the three cores rose thousands of degrees, melting the fuel rods and causing explosions over the next few days. The release of radioactive materials led to the immediate evacuation of everyone living within 12 miles (19 km) of the plant. Eventually, people living within 18 miles (29 km) of the power plant were evacuated too. Altogether, the evacuations included four hundred thousand people. Years later, some areas are still not safe enough to inhabit. Almost fifty thousand people still can't return home.

Experts predict that increases in thyroid cancer and leukemia similar to what doctors observed after Chernobyl will occur in Japan. The full extent of the Fukushima disaster won't be known for many years.

Decontamination started soon after the wave hit the plant. On April 10, 2011, teams used heavy remote-controlled equipment to clean up radioactive debris and rubble surrounding the reactors. They placed contaminated garbage in large on-site containers. Sensors all around the nuclear plant detect radioactive isotopes in the soil, water, and air.

By late 2014, radiation levels in the reactor buildings had lowered enough for workers to remove the spent fuel rods at the plant safely. By 2017 contamination and radiation was no longer escaping from the power plant. With the help of swimming robot investigators and special probes, researchers have begun to find melted core in reactor debris. Removing this material will be very difficult.

Farmers in the Fukushima area grow rice, which is tested for radiation. All the Fukushima rice has passed the Japanese national safety standards. The three nuclear cores are still dangerously hot. None of the cooling pipes is intact, and the cores are still too radioactive for humans to install new cooling systems in the molten mess. So cooling water is sprayed over the three reactors. Through complex filtering systems, the plant has removed sixty-two different radioactive isotopes from the contaminated cooling water. But the systems don't capture radioactive tritium (H-3), so workers can't release the water into the ocean. Instead, more than 1 million tons (907,000 t) of water is stored on-site. Every day workers add 100 tons (91 t) of water.

The Japanese government estimates the final bill for the complete cleanup will be at least $188 billion. The effort will last at least another thirty years.

NUCLEAR ENERGY IN THE TWENTY-FIRST CENTURY

Altogether, about 440 nuclear power plants among thirty-one countries supply about 11 percent of the world's electricity. The United States, France, Russia, and China have nuclear power plants. Building a nuclear power plant is expensive—$10 billion or more— and the plants generate long-term radioactive waste. Disastrous accidents are a risk, and it is very expensive to dismantle a power plant once it has passed its expected life span of forty to seventy years. So it is unlikely that the United States will build more nuclear power plants. The US Nuclear Regulatory Commission oversees all the nuclear power plants in the United States. It inspects all operating nuclear plants and issues a forty-year operating license. The commission conducts more than one thousand inspections a year. Seventy-four of the ninety-nine operating nuclear power plants in the United States have been operating longer than the licensed period. The commission has granted them another twenty years of operation. Yet when the plants were built, operators expected that all spent nuclear fuel could go to Yucca Mountain in Nevada for burial. Until that happens, US nuclear waste is being stored locally.

Due to the high cost and dangers associated with nuclear power, most developed countries are no longer building new nuclear power plants. But Russia, China, and South Korea are building new plants. Japan shut down every one of its forty-three nuclear power plants after the Fukushima disaster. In 2018 five of the reactors are running again, but public opinion will prevent many more from operating again. German chancellor Angela Merkel has pledged to shut down that nation's twenty-two nuclear power plants by 2022.

WHAT CAN YOU DO?

Meeting the world's energy needs is challenging. Many nations are working to reduce greenhouse gas emissions to slow global warming. Others are moving away from fossil fuels and turning to alternative sources to provide energy in safe, renewable ways. Still others are pulling away from nuclear energy. Is nuclear power a

FUSION FOR ENERGY

The sun's energy comes from fusion reactions. Fusion reactions involve the combination of small nuclei (hydrogen and helium). Scientists are very interested in trying to duplicate this in nuclear fusion reactors. The International Thermonuclear Experimental Reactor in the south of France and the Experimental Advanced Superconducting Tokamak reactor in China are two major experimental fusion projects. Each is generating temperatures of over 180 million°F (100 million°C) to fuse hydrogen-2 and hydrogen-3 nuclei to produce helium-4. The facilities are complicated and expensive. So far, they haven't been able to keep fusion reactions going for longer than one hundred seconds. It will be many years before it will be possible to create electricity from fusion reactors.

smart way for a nation to meet its energy needs? Here are some things you can research further and discuss with family, friends, and classmates as you think about nuclear energy:

- Unless there is another nuclear disaster, your biggest exposure to radiation is likely to be radon. The EPA has determined that radon is the second-leading cause of lung cancer. Radon is a radioactive gas. You can't see it or smell it. It gives off alpha particles and has a half-life of 3.8 days. Because it is a gas, humans inhale it into the lungs where it causes damage. The EPA estimates that unhealthy levels of radon are present in eight million US homes, causing twenty thousand lung cancer deaths a year. It is typically in basements and well water. Encourage your parents to do an easy home radon test. Kits are available at hardware stores and usually cost no more than twenty to forty dollars. It is the only way to detect radon. If your house has unhealthy levels of radon, run a second test before choosing an EPA-recommended radon-removal system.
- What do you think about US nuclear power plants? They provide a lot of energy without producing greenhouse gases. But nuclear power plants generate radioactive waste that's difficult to store safely. And the risk of a disaster is always there. Fossil fuels, solar, and wind power plants don't have this risk. Are the risks worth the benefits?

You can be part of the solution to global energy challenges. You can reduce your carbon footprint by reducing your energy use, avoiding single-use plastics, and reducing the amount of things you buy. Educate yourself about the issues and the science underlying them. Talk to your family and friends about them. Volunteer in your community to clean up trash along the roadways and coastlines. Write to or work with leaders in your community to make green solutions happen. Start a youth group with your friends and classmates. You can make a difference.

GREEN TEENS

Teens around the world are working to make a difference. Here are just three examples of green teens:

Hannah Alper. A Canadian blogger, environmental activist, author, and motivational speaker, Hannah Alper is the only teenager on Bloomberg's Ones to Watch 2018 list. The previous year, in 2017, her book *Momentus: Small Acts, Big Change* was published. A Toronto, Ontario, native, she believes that "if there are many of us making small actions, it will lead to big change." Besides blogging and writing, she has organized a shoreline cleanup in her community and has been a team captain for the World Wildlife Federation Earth Hour.

Kehkashan Basu. When she was sixteen, Kehkashan Basu won the International Children's Peace Prize. She was born in the United Arab Emirates to Indian parents and lives in Dubai. Nkosi Johnson, a South African AIDs activist, and Pakistani education advocate Malala Yousafzai are previous awardees. In 2012, when she was twelve years old, Kehkashan founded Green Hope Foundation to help build a sustainable future through direct action. Within four years, the youth organization grew to more than one thousand members in ten countries. Green Hope volunteers have planted thousands of trees in the United States, France, Nepal, Mexico, and Colombia.

Xiuhtezcatl Roske-Martinez. Boulder, Colorado, native Xiuhtezcatl Roske-Martinez comes from a family of environmental activists and got an early start. He started advocating for the environment when he was six years old. By 2017 he had given a TED talk, been on President Barack Obama's Youth Council, was among twenty-one youth plaintiffs to sue the US government for not acting on climate change, and had given a speech to the United Nations. He is the youth director of a worldwide conservation organization, called Earth Guardians. In fall 2017, he published his first book, *We Rise: The Earth Guardians Guide to Building a Movement That Restores the Planet.*

SOURCE NOTES

18 Colin Baird and Michael Cann, *Environmental Chemistry*, 5th ed. (W. H. Freeman, New York), 574.

29 Allan H. Smith, Elena O. Lingas, and Mahfuzar Rahman, "Contamination of Drinking-Water by Arsenic in Bangladesh: A Public Health Emergency," *Bulletin of the World Health Organization* 78, no. 9 (2000): 1093.

35 John Keats, "La Belle Dame sans Merci," original version, in *Selected Poems and Letters*, ed. Douglas Bush (Boston: Houghton Mifflin, 1959), 199–202.

36–37 Eliza Griswold, "How *Silent Spring* Ignited the Environmental Movement," *New York Times Magazine*, September 21, 2012, https://www.nytimes.com/2012/09/23/magazine/how-silent-spring-ignited-the-environmental-movement.html.

37 Homer, *The Odyssey*, trans. Robert Fitzgerald (New York: Doubleday, 1961), 463.

38 "Paul Hermann Müller," *World of Anatomy and Physiology* (Detroit: Gale, 2006), online at http://link.galegroup.com/apps/doc/K2430100143/SCIC?u=connc_main&sid=SCIC&xid=95127ae6.

38 Paul Müller Nobel Lecture, 1948, Nobelprize.org, accessed June 10, 2018, https://www.nobelprize.org/nobel_prizes/medicine/laureates/1948/muller-lecture.pdf.

39 Announcement for the Nobel Prize in Physiology or Medicine 1948, Nobelprize.org, accessed June 10, 2018, https://www.nobelprize.org/nobel_prizes/medicine/laureates/1948/.

39 G. Fischer, Award Ceremony Speech, presentation speech, Nobel Prize in Medicine, 1948, Nobelprize.org, accessed June 10, 2018, https://www.nobelprize.org/nobel_prizes/medicine/laureates/1948/press.html.

40 "What Are POPs?," Stockholm Convention, 2008, accessed June 10, 2018, http://chm.pops.int/TheConvention/ThePOPs/tabid/673/Default.aspx.

65 Brian Kahn, "The World Passes 400 ppm Threshold. Permanently," Climate Central, June 15, 2016, http://www.climatecentral.org/news/world-passes-400-ppm-threshold-permanently-20738.

90 Announcement for the Nobel Prize in Chemistry, 1911, Nobelprize.org, accessed June 9, 2018, https://www.nobelprize.org/nobel_prizes/chemistry/laureates/1911/.

109 Becky Hughes, "15-Year-Old Activist Hannah Alper Is 'One to Watch' in 2018," *Parade*, February 2, 2018, https://parade.com/642629/beckyhughes/15-year-old-activist-hannah-alper-is-one-to-watch-in-2018/.

GLOSSARY

acute exposure: a short-term exposure to a toxin. It is often due to a single release of a pollutant in an accident or spill.

anthropogenic: something caused by human activity

atom: the defining structure of an element. Each atom has a nucleus composed of protons and neutrons that is surrounded by electrons

atomic mass number (A): the mass of all the protons and neutrons in the nucleus of an element

bioaccumulation: the accumulation of a chemical in a living organism so that the concentration of the compound is higher in the organism than its surroundings

biofuel: a fuel such as wood or ethanol that is derived directly from living matter

biomagnification: the increase in concentration of a pollutant in organisms at increasingly higher levels of the food chain

centrifugation: spinning a solution of liquid or gas so fast that the force of spinning (centrifugal force) separates the components of the solution

chain reaction: a self-sustaining sequence of reactions that once started will continue going, by each reaction starting a new one

chronic exposure: a long-term exposure to a toxin or pollutant. This is often a continuous or repeated exposure that occurs over months or years.

climate change: long-term changes in climate caused by increases in greenhouse gases in Earth's atmosphere. Most climate changes involve increases in temperature and more extreme weather conditions such as rain and wind.

compound: a chemical composed of at least two different elements

deoxyribonucleic acid (DNA): hereditary or genetic material found in all living organisms

dichloro-diphenyl-trichloroethane (DDT): a toxic insecticide. It is globally prohibited, except to control *Anopheles* mosquitoes, which can transmit malaria.

diffusion: the net movement of molecules from a region of high concentration to a region of low concentration as a result of random motion of the molecules

doping: adding impurities into a pure substance to change the chemical properties of the material

electromagnetic radiation: a kind of radiation and a form of energy that includes radio waves, infrared, visible light, ultraviolet, gamma rays, and X-rays

electron: a negatively charged particle in an atom. Protons (positively charged) and electrons have equal but opposite charges.

element: a type of atom. So far, scientists know of 118 elements. They all have different numbers of protons.

enrichment: increasing the percentage of uranium-235 in a sample

environmental chemistry: using chemistry to understand the harmful effects humans have on the environment

extreme weather: weather that is very different from normal weather patterns and behavior and causes more damage than usual. It includes intense hurricanes and rainstorms, heavy snowstorms and flooding, and devastating drought. Damage from extreme weather is into the millions and billions of dollars and is often responsible for many human deaths.

fossil fuel: a fuel such as coal, natural gas, or petroleum formed by the long-term decay of the remains of ancient plants, animals, and marine organisms

genetic modification (GM): the addition of a foreign gene into the DNA of an organism to alter its characteristics

greenhouse effect: the warming of Earth's atmosphere by an increase in gases such as methane and carbon dioxide that trap heat. The greenhouse effect is linked to global warming and climate change.

greenhouse gas: a gas, such as carbon dioxide and methane, that traps heat in the atmosphere. These gases have three or more atoms. Their vibrations absorb infrared radiation (heat), and the growing levels of greenhouse gases in the atmosphere contribute to global warming and climate change.

half-life: the time it takes the radiation of a radioactive element to reach half its starting level of radiation

horizontal drilling: drilling parallel to Earth's surface as one way to mine difficult-to-reach fossil fuels

hybrid car: a car with a number of different power sources, such as gas and electricity

hydraulic fracturing (fracking): a drilling technique that involves a high-pressure injection of fluids (water and lubricating materials) into a well to create cracks through which natural gas and petroleum will flow. Fracking wells are often drilled parallel to the surface in deep underground rock formations.

isotope: atoms of the same element that have the same number of protons but differing numbers of neutrons

kinetic energy: the energy an object has due to its movement

lethal dose 50 (LD_{50}): the amount of toxic material that causes the death of 50 percent of a group of test animals

maximum contaminant level (MCL): the highest level of a contaminant allowed in drinking water

metal: a solid that is typically hard and shiny and that conducts electricity. Metals are on the left side of the periodic table.

metalloid: elements that resemble both metals and nonmetals. They look like metals and they are shiny, but they behave like nonmetals because they don't conduct electricity and are brittle.

metamorphosis: the transformation of an insect from an immature form of life (such as a larva) to an adult form (such as a butterfly). The cycle of transformation includes at least two distinct phases.

molecule: a group of atoms that have bound together

neutron: a particle with no charge. Together with protons, neutrons form the nucleus of an atom.

nonmetal: elements on the right-hand side of the periodic table that are not metals

nuclear chemistry: the study of the chemistry of the nucleus of an atom

nuclear fission: the reaction that occurs when a large unstable nucleus spontaneously falls apart forming new smaller nuclei and releasing energy

nuclear fusion: the merging of small nuclei to form a larger nucleus. The process releases energy.

nuclear meltdown: severe damage to the reactor core at a nuclear power station due to overheating

organic compound: a compound of nonmetals with carbon atoms forming a central ring or chainlike structure

particulate matter (PM): a complex mixture of extremely small solid particles and liquid droplets suspended in the air

parts per million (ppm): a way of expressing the concentration of solutions or gases. The measurement shows how many pollutant molecules are in one million molecules of the solution or gas.

periodic table: an infographic with columns that organize elements according to the number of protons in their nucleus and their chemical properties

persistent organic pollutant (POP): a toxic organic compound that remains intact for years, that biomagnifies, and that is distributed all over the world (mainly in the air)

pesticide: a substance used to prevent, destroy, or repel a pest

photoconversion: when a photovoltaic cell absorbs visible and ultraviolet radiation to excite electrons to create electricity

photosynthesis: green plants and other organisms using carbon dioxide, water, and energy from sunlight to make sugars and oxygen

photovoltaic technology: the production of electricity from sunlight

proton: a positively charged particle found in the nucleus of an atom. Each atom has an equal number of electrons and protons.

radioisotope: an isotope with an unstable nucleus. It undergoes radioactive decay and emits alpha, beta, or gamma radiation to gain stability.

sarcophagus: a large metal and concrete structure built over a destroyed nuclear reactor to prevent the radioactive isotopes from entering the environment

sink: something that removes a pollutant from the environment. Sinks include plants that absorb carbon dioxide to photosynthesize and the soil, which can incorporate many heavy metals.

source: something that adds a pollutant to the environment. Sources include car exhausts that release particulate matter and smokestacks that release carbon dioxide. When the size of a source is equal to a sink, the concentration of the pollutant is constant. If the source is larger than the sink, the concentration of the pollutant increases.

species-specific insecticide: a pesticide that negatively impacts the population of a single targeted species of insects without harming other species

spectroscopy: the study of the absorption and emission of radiation by chemical compounds

sterile insect technique: mass rearing of insects to sterilize the males and release the sterilized males in the wild so that they outnumber fertile males. If a female mates with a sterile male, she won't produce offspring. Over time, if enough females mate with sterile males, the population of that insect collapses.

SELECTED BIBLIOGRAPHY

Baird, Colin, and Michael Cann. *Environmental Chemistry.* 5th ed. New York: W. H. Freeman, 2012.

Middlecamp, Catherine H., Michael T. Mury, Karen L. Anderson, Anne K. Bentley, Michael C. Cann, Jamie P. Ellis, and Kathleen L. Purvis-Roberts. *Chemistry in Context.* 8th ed. New York: McGraw-Hill Education, 2017.

VanLoon, Gary W., and Stephen J. Duffy. *Environmental Chemistry: A Global Perspective.* 3rd ed. Oxford: Oxford Univerity Press, 2011.

FURTHER INFORMATION

Books

Bortz, Fred. *Meltdown! The Nuclear Disaster in Japan and Our Energy Future.* Minneapolis: Twenty-First Century Books, 2012.

Brown, Lester. *The Great Transition: Shifting from Fossil Fuels to Solar and Wind Energy.* New York: W. W. Norton, 2015.

Carson, Rachel. Silent Spring *& Other Environmental Writings.* New York: Library of America, 2018.

Di Piazza, Francesca Davis. *Remaking the John: The Invention and Reinvention of the Toilet.* Minneapolis: Twenty-First Century Books, 2015.

Flaubert, Gustave. *Madame Bovary.* Translated by Lowell Bair. New York: Penguin Books, 2015.

Francis, Amy. *Wind Farms*. Farmington Hills, MI: Greenhaven, 2015.

Goldstein, Margaret J. *Fuel under Fire: Petroleum and Its Perils*. Minneapolis: Twenty-First Century Books, 2016.

Griswold, Eliza. *Amity and Prosperity: One Family and the Fracturing of America*. New York: Farrar, Straus & Giroux, 2018.

Hirsch, Rebecca E. *Climate Migrants: On the Move in a Warming World*. Minneapolis: Twenty-First Century Books, 2017.

Johnson, Rebecca L. *Chernobyl's Wild Kingdom: Life in the Dead Zone*. Minneapolis: Twenty-First Century Books, 2015.

Kallen, Stuart A. *Running Dry: The Global Water Crisis*. Minneapolis: Twenty-First Century Books, 2015.

Lafarge, Marie. *Memoirs of Madame Lafarge*. 2 vols. Reprint, London: Forgotten Books, 2018.

McPherson, Stephanie Sammartino. *Arctic Thaw: Climate Change and the Global Race for Energy Resources*. Minneapolis: Twenty-First Century Books, 2015.

Redniss, Lauren. *Radioactive: Marie & Pierre Curie; A Tale of Love and Fallout*. New York: HarperCollins, 2011.

Zimmer, Marc. *Bioluminescence: Nature and Science at Work*. Minneapolis: Twenty-First Century Books, 2016.

———. *Lighting Up the Brain: The Science of Optogenetics*. Minneapolis: Twenty-First Century Books, 2018.

Videos

"Best of Intentions." 12:35. Posted by "messymomentmedia," May 7, 2015. https://www.youtube.com/watch?v=1WLDulkwsXY.
This television report from *60 Minutes* on the Bangladeshi arsenic poisoning discusses the biggest mass poisoning in history.

"Climate Change: Oh, It's Real"
https://www.ted.com/playlists/78/climate_change_oh_it_s_real
This series of TED Talks focuses on climate change. The talks range from four minutes to half an hour and feature speakers such as top climate scientist James Hansen and former US vice president, author, and climate activist Al Gore.

"Corrosive Chemistry: How Lead Ended Up in Flint's Drinking Water." 1:59. *Scientific American*. https://www.scientificamerican.com/video/corrosive-chemistry-how-lead-ended-up-in-flint-s-drinking-water1/.
This animated video explains the chemistry responsible for lead dissolving into Flint's water supply.

"How Does Fracking Work? TED-Ed." 5:51. Posted by Lock the Gate Alliance, August 14, 2017. https://www.youtube.com/watch?v=0hLj1NQriIM. TED-Ed videos are short video lessons aimed at educators and students. This animated video shows how fracking removes methane from deep shale beds and why this technology is so controversial.

"How Safe Are Pesticides Really?" 12:15. Posted by SciShow, June 13, 2018. https://www.youtube.com/watch?v=eF_fbTbHdyg. This video presents both the advantages and disadvantages of pesticides. It also contrasts the dangers of natural and synthetic pesticides and describes how to wash pesticides off our foods.

"How to Visualize One Part per Million." 2:27. TED-Ed. https://ed.ted.com/lessons/how-to-visualize-one-part-per-million-kim-preshoff-the-ted-ed-community#watch. This animated video presents nine ways of visualizing the concept of parts per million.

Periodic Videos: TED-Ed https://ed.ted.com/periodic-videos See videos for Hg (mercury), Pb (lead), and As (arsenic). This series of videos produced by the University of Nottingham describes the properties of all the elements.

"Renewable Energy 101." 3:16. Posted by *National Geographic*, September 21, 2017. https://www.youtube.com/watch?v=1kUEOBZtTRc. *National Geographic* answers the question "What is renewable energy?" in a well-balanced video showing both the advantages and disadvantages of the fastest-growing energy resource in the world.

Website

"Renewable Energy Explained": US Energy Information Administration https://www.eia.gov/energyexplained/?page=renewable_home. This comprehensive website discusses renewable energy, its role in the United States, and descriptions of the five most common renewable energies (biomass, solar, wind, hydro, and geothermal) and has many useful infographics.

INDEX

PHOTO ACKNOWLEDGMENTS

Image credits: NASA/abbreviation of appropriate center, for example NASA/JPL, NASA/ARC, etc, p. 4; Laura Westlund/Independent Picture Service, pp. 5, 7, 18, 20, 31, 36, 52, 59, 63, 66, 70, 71, 77, 82–83, 92, 97; Archive Photos/Getty Images, p. 6; Mikael Häggström/Wikimedia Commons (CC0 1.0), p. 11; AP Photo//Chitose Suzuki, p. 13; © BP Magazine, advert, UK, 1930s/The Advertising Archives/Bridgeman Images, p. 16; Bettmann/Getty Images, p. 19; LindaParton/iStock Editorial/Getty Images, p. 22; John Springer Collection/Corbis/Getty Images, p. 27; REUTERS// Rafiqur Rahman, p. 30; STRDEL/AFP/Getty Images, p. 33; Alfred Eisenstaedt/The LIFE Picture Collection/Getty Images, p. 34; NYPL/Science Source/Getty Images, p. 38; Wolfgang Kaehler/LightRocket/Getty Images, p. 40; Courtesy of Science History Institute/Wikimedia Commons (PD), p. 41; Universal Images Group North America LLC/Alamy Stock Photo, p. 44; Grant Heilman Photography/Alamy Stock Photo, p. 46; AusAID/Alamy Stock Photo, p. 49; Kevin Frayer/Getty Images, p. 51; In Pictures Ltd./Corbis/Getty Images, p. 55; Mikkel Rønne/Moment/Getty Images, p, 65; chain45154/Getty Images, p. 67; Jose Luis Pelaez/Getty Images, p. 69; U.S. Energy Information Administration/Monthly Energy Review, p. 76; Stuart Dee/Getty Images, p. 78; GIPhotoStock/Getty Images, p. 81; Courtesy of Domenica DiPiazza, p. 86; Mansell/Mansell/The LIFE Picture Collection/Getty Images, p. 88; Universal History Archive/Getty Images, p. 88; Popperfoto/Getty Images, p. 89; Picavet/Getty Images, p. 95; GENYA SAVILOV/AFP/Getty Images, p. 103; Christopher Furlong/ Getty Images, p. 104.

Cover Images: Sergey Nivens/Shutterstock.com (graphic); Only Fabrizio/ Shutterstock.com (leaves).

ABOUT THE AUTHOR

Marc Zimmer is a professor of chemistry at Connecticut College, where he teaches general chemistry, molecular science, and environmental chemistry. His research focuses on understanding and designing brighter fluorescent proteins. He has written two books for adults about green fluorescent proteins. For YA readers, he is the author of *Bioluminescence: Nature and Science at Work* and *Lighting Up the Brain: The Science of Optogenetics*.

Zimmer's articles about green fluorescent proteins have appeared in *USA Today*, the *Los Angeles Times*, and other publications. He hosts a green fluorescent proteins website (https://gfp.conncoll.edu/) and gives talks about them to groups around the world. At Connecticut College and as part of the Semester at Sea study abroad program, Zimmer regularly teaches classes about bioluminescence and its applications in medical research.

Zimmer got his PhD at Worcester Polytechnic Institute in Massachusetts and did his postdoctoral studies at Yale University. He loves teaching and has won a variety of teaching awards. To stay amused and intrigued, Zimmer takes on unique studies, such as analyzing the formation of cow flatulence, which contributes to the buildup of the greenhouse gas methane in Earth's atmosphere.